Accounting for Non-Accountants

Accounting for Non-Accountants

The fast and easy way to learn the basics

DR. WAYNE A. LABEL, CPA

SOURCEBOOKS, INC.®
NAPERVILLE, ILLINOIS

Published by Sourcebooks, Inc.
P.O. Box 4410, Naperville, Illinois 60567-4410
(630) 961-3900
FAX: (630) 961-2168
www.sourcebooks.com

Library of Congress Cataloging-in-Publication Data
Label, Wayne A. (Wayne Allan)
  Accounting for non-accountants : the fast and easy way to learn the basics / Wayne
Label.
       p. cm.
  Includes bibliographical references and index.
  ISBN-13: 978-1-4022-0657-3
  ISBN-10: 1-4022-0657-7
  1. Accounting. 2. Financial statements. I. Title. II. Title: Accounting for nonaccoun-
tants.

HF5636.L33 2006
657—dc22

                                                                2006012421

Printed and bound in the United States of America.
VP 10 9 8 7 6

Contents

- The Parts of the Report
- Other Types of Audit Reports
- Why Audits Are Useful to You

Acknowledgments

I would like to thank Ewurama Ewusi-Mensah and Rachel Jay at Sourcebooks for their tireless efforts to make this book readable and understandable to the non-accountants of the world.

I would also like to thank Drs. Bruce Lubich and Richard Samuelson for their time and effort in reading the manuscript, adding valuable insights, and making the book a better read.

Finally, I would like to thank the thousands of students and users of my previous book on this same topic whose comments and suggestions have helped to improve this book.

Introduction

What is accounting? Who needs it? How does it benefit businesses? This book answers those questions for the non-accountant.

Accounting provides information that helps people in business increase their chances of making decisions that will benefit their companies. Accounting is the language of business, and like other languages, it has its own terms and rules. Understanding this language and learning to interpret it is your first step to becoming successful in your own business and in your personal financial life as well.

In your personal life you can use accounting information to make decisions about investing in the stock market, applying for a loan, and evaluating potential jobs. Banks use accounting information to make decisions about granting loans. Government agencies base their regulations on accounting information. Accounting information can even be useful to non-business entities with an interest in how businesses affect local, national, or foreign communities and community members. Businesses use accounting information for planning and budgeting and for making decisions about borrowing and investing. Overall, accounting aids businesses in the process of making better decisions.

The basics of accounting are the same regardless of the size or type of business. In *Accounting for Non-Accountants*, you will learn the basics of accounting through the examination of an imaginary small business, Solana Beach Bicycle Company. For more complex businesses, the economic transactions become more varied and complex as does the process of reporting them to various users. The foundation of it all, however, remains the same. This book will give you a solid foundation you will be able to use in any accounting situation you encounter.

Whether you own a business or do not, even if you've never had any experience with accounting and financial statements, this is the book for you.

I hope that you find this book useful in helping you to understand these accounting issues as they apply to your small business and to your personal life. Please feel free to contact me at wayne@waynelabel.com with your thoughts on the book.

Chapter 1

Introducing Accounting and Financial Statements

▶ **What Is Accounting?**

▶ **Who Uses Accounting Information?**

▶ **Financial Statements**

▶ **How Different Business Entities Present Accounting Information**

What Is Accounting?

The purpose of accounting is to provide information that will help you make correct financial decisions. Your accountant's job is to give you the information you need to run your business as efficiently as possible while maximizing profits and keeping costs low.

QUICK Tip

Finding an Accountant: Hiring a professional and ethical accountant to aid in your business operations can be critical to the success of your company. Meet with a few accountants before making a final choice so that you know your options and can select one whose experience and work style will be best suited to your needs and the needs of your business. Local chapters of your state societies of CPAs offer referral services that can help with this.

Accounting plays a role in businesses of all sizes. Your kids' lemonade stand, a one-person business, and a multinational corporation all use the same basic accounting principles. Accounting is legislated; it affects your taxes; even the president plays a role in how accounting affects you. The list goes on and on.

Accounting is the language of business. It is the process of recording, classifying, and summarizing economic events through certain documents or financial statements. Like any other language, accounting has its own terms and rules. To understand how to interpret and use the information accounting provides, you must first understand this language. Understanding the basic concepts of accounting is essential to success in business.

Different types of information furnished by accountants are shown in Figure 1.1 on the next page.

Figure 1.1: **TYPES OF INFORMATION PROVIDED BY ACCOUNTANTS**

- Information prepared exclusively by people within a company (managers, employees, or owners) for their own use.
- Financial information required by various government agencies such as the Internal Revenue Service (IRS), Securities and Exchange Commission (SEC), and the Federal Trade Commission (FTC).
- General information about companies provided to people outside the firm such as investors, creditors, and labor unions.

Accounting and Bookkeeping

Bookkeeping procedures and bookkeepers record and keep track of the business transactions that are later used to generate financial statements. Most bookkeeping procedures have been systematized, and, in many cases, can be handled by computer programs. Bookkeeping is a very important part of the accounting process, but it is just the beginning. There is currently no certification required to become a bookkeeper in the United States.

Accounting is the process of preparing and analyzing financial statements based on the transactions recorded through the bookkeeping process. Accountants are usually professionals who have completed at least a bachelor's degree in accounting, and often have passed a professional examination, like the Certified Public Accountant Examination, the Certified Management Accountant Examination, or the Certified Fraud Auditor Examination.

Accounting goes beyond bookkeeping and the recording of economic information to include the summarizing and reporting of this information in a way that is meant to drive decision making within a business.

Who Uses Accounting Information?

In the world of business, accounting plays an important role to aid in making critical decisions. The more complex the decision, the more detailed the information must be. Individuals and companies need different kinds of information to make their business decisions.

Let's start with you as an individual. Why would you be interested in accounting? Accounting knowledge can help you with investing in the stock market, applying for a home loan, evaluating a potential job, balancing a checkbook, and starting a personal savings plan, among other things.

Managers within a business also use accounting information daily to make decisions, although most of these managers are not accountants. Some of the decisions they might make for which they will use accounting information are illustrated below in Figure 1.2

Figure 1.2: AREAS IN WHICH MANAGERS USE ACCOUNTING INFORMATION

- Marketing (Which line of goods should the company emphasize?)
- Production (Should the company produce its goods in the United States or open a new plant in Mexico?)
- Research and Development (How much money should be set aside for new product development?)
- Sales (Should the company expand the advertising budget and take money away from some other part of the marketing budget?)

Without the proper accounting information these types of decisions would be very difficult, if not impossible, to make.

Bankers continually use accounting information. They are in the business of taking care of your money and making money with your money, so they absolutely must make good decisions. Accounting is fundamental to their decision-making process. Figure 1.3 looks at some of the decisions bankers make using accounting information.

Figure 1.3: AREAS IN WHICH BANKERS USE ACCOUNTING INFORMATION

- Granting loans to individuals and companies
- Investing clients' money
- Setting interest rates
- Meeting federal regulations for protecting your money

Government agencies such as the Internal Revenue Service (IRS), the Securities and Exchange Commission (SEC), the Federal Trade Commission (FTC), and the Bureau of Alcohol, Tobacco, and Firearms (ATF) base their regulation enforcement and compliance on the accounting information they receive.

Accountability in Accounting

A business's financial statements can also be of great interest to other members of the local or national community. Labor groups might be interested in what impact management's financial decisions have on their unions and other employees. Local communities have an interest in how a business's financial decisions (for example, layoffs or plant closings) will impact their citizens.

As the economy becomes more complex, so do the transactions within a business, and the process of reporting them to various users and making them understandable becomes more complex as well. A solid knowledge of accounting is helpful to individuals, managers, and business owners who are making their decisions based on the information accounting documents provide.

Financial Statements

Accountants supply information to people both inside and outside the firm by issuing formal reports that are called financial statements.

The financial statements are usually issued at least once a year. In many cases they are issued quarterly or more often where necessary. A set of rules, called Generally Accepted Accounting Principles, govern the preparation of the financial statements. Generally Accepted Accounting Principles (GAAP) has been defined as a set of objectives, conventions, and principles to govern the preparation and presentation of financial statements. These rules can be found in volumes of documents issued by the American Institute of Certified Public Accountants (AICPA), the Financial Accounting Standards Board (FASB), the Internal Revenue Service (IRS), the Securities and Exchange Commission (SEC), and other regulatory bodies. In chapter 2 we look at some of the overriding principles of accounting as they apply to all businesses and individuals.

The Basic Financial Statements

The basic financial statements include the Balance Sheet, the Income Statement, the Statement of Cash Flows, and the Statement of Retained Earnings. We will look at these in depth in the following chapters and see how they all interact with each other. As we discuss these financial statements, you will see they are not as scary as you might have thought they would be. Many of the concepts will already be familiar to you.

In the appendix, you can see examples of these financial statements from Station Casinos, Inc., a publicly traded company which operates several casinos and hotels in the Las Vegas, Nevada, area.

The Balance Sheet is the statement that presents the Assets of the company (those items owned by the company) and the Liabilities (those items owed to others by the company).

The Income Statement shows all of the Revenues of the company less the Expenses, to arrive at the "bottom line," the Net Income.

The Statement of Cash Flows shows how much cash we started the period with, what additions and subtractions were made during the period, and how much cash we have left over at the end of the period.

The Statement of Retained Earnings shows how the balance in Retained Earnings has changed during the period of time (year, quarter, month) for which the financial statements are being prepared. Normally there are only two types of events that will cause the beginning balance to change: 1) the company makes a profit, which causes an increase in Retained Earnings (or the company suffers a loss, which would cause a decrease) and 2) the owners of the company withdraw money, which causes the beginning balance to decrease (or invest more money, which will cause it to increase).

Seeing the Bigger Picture: None of these financial statements alone can tell the whole story about a company. We need to know how to read, understand, and analyze these statements as a package in order to make any kind of decisions about the company. In addition to the financial statements, you must understand the industry you are operating in and the general economy.

Financial statements vary in form depending upon the type of business they are used in. In general there are three forms of business operating in the United States—proprietorships, partnerships, and corporations.

How Different Business Entities Present Accounting Information

Proprietorships are businesses with a single owner like you and me. These types of businesses tend to be small retail businesses started by entrepreneurs. The accounting for these proprietorships includes only the records of the business—not the personal financial records of the proprietor of the business.

Don't Mix and Match: The financial records of an individual owner of a business should never be combined with those of the business. They are two separate entities and need to be accounted for separately. Taking money from one of these entities (the business) for the other (the owner), must be accounted for by both entities.

Partnerships are very similar to proprietorships, except that instead of one owner, there are two or more owners. In general most of these businesses are small to medium-sized. However, there are some exceptions, such as large national or even international accounting or law firms that may have thousands of partners. As with the proprietorships, accounting treats these organizations' records as separate and distinct from those of the individual partners.

Finally, there are corporations. These are businesses that are owned by one or more stockholders. These owners may or may not have a managerial interest in the company. Many of these stockholders are simply private citizens who have money invested in the company by way of stocks that they have purchased.

In a corporation a person becomes an owner by buying shares in the company and thus becomes a stockholder. The stockholders may or may not have a vote in the company's long-term planning depending on the type of stock they have purchased. However, simply by being stockholders (owners), they do not have decision-making authority in the day-to-day operations. These investors (or stockholders) are not much different than the bankers that loan money to a proprietorship or a partnership. These bankers have a financial interest in the business, but no daily managerial decision-making power. As is the case with the stockholders who have invested money into the corporation, in general they have a nonmanagerial interest in the business. As with the other two types of business organizations discussed here, the accounting records of the corporation are maintained separately from those of the individual stockholders or owners.

The accounting records of a proprietorship are less complex than those of a corporation in that there is a simple capital structure and only one owner. In the case of a corporation, there are stockholders who buy a piece of the ownership of a company by buying stock. As we will discuss later, because of this stock ownership, the financial statements become more complex. Some of the basic differences between these three types of businesses are shown in Figure 1.4.

Figure 1.4: **DIFFERENCES IN THE THREE TYPES OF BUSINESSES**

Business Type	Proprietorship	Partnership	Corporation
Number of Owners	One	Two or more	One or more
Accounting Records	Maintained separately from owner's records	Maintained separately from owner's records	Maintained separately from owner's records
Owner Has Managerial Responsibilities	Yes	Usually	Usually not

In this chapter you have learned what accounting is, why you and other people in business need to understand accounting, what businesses use accounting for, and what the basic financial statements used in these businesses are. In chapter 2 you will learn about the practical and ethical principles accountants use on a regular basis.

GLOSSARY

Accounting: The process of recording, classifying, and summarizing economic events through the preparation of financial statements such as the Balance Sheet, the Income Statement, and the Statement of Cash Flows.

American Institute of Certified Public Accountants (AICPA): The professional organization of CPAs in the United States. The AICPA is charged with preparation of the CPA Examination, the establishment and enforcement of the code of professional ethics, and working with the Financial Accounting Standards Board in the proclamation of accounting standards.

Corporations: Corporations are businesses that are given the right to exist by an individual state in the United States. With this right to exist, the corporation is then allowed to sell stock. Those buying this stock become owners of the corporation. Corporations can be set up as for profit or not for profit, and make that decision when applying for their charter with the state.

Financial Accounting Standards Board (FASB): The FASB sets the accounting standards to be followed for the preparation of financial statements. All rulings from the FASB are considered to be GAAP.

Financial Statements: Reports prepared by companies on the financial status of their business; examples are Balance Sheets, Income Statements, Statement of Cash Flow, and Statement of Retained Earnings.

Generally Accepted Accounting Principles (GAAP): The rules that govern the preparation of financial statements. These rules are developed by the American Institute of Certified Public Accountants, the Financial Accounting Standards Board, the Security and Exchange Commission, and other government agencies.

Internal Revenue Service (IRS): The government agency charged with the collection of federal taxes in the United States. There are different accounting rules for the preparation of taxes in the United States than for the presentation of financial statements.

Partnerships: A business entity with two or more owners. The accounting for partnerships is similar to that of proprietorships.

Proprietorships, Sole Proprietorships: Businesses with one single owner. Even though there is only one owner, the records of the owner's personal financial affairs are kept separate from those of the accounting records of the business. Separate tax returns are prepared for the business and for the individual.

Chapter 2

Generally Accepted Accounting Principles

▶ **Who Are the SEC, AICPA, and the FASB?**

▶ **Generally Accepted Accounting Principles (GAAP)**

is important that you understand the concepts of Generally Accepted
unting Principles (GAAP), which form the basis of accounting and are
part of the language of accounting and business.

This chapter will introduce the agencies responsible for standardizing the
accounting principles that are used in the United States and it will describe
those principles in full detail. Once you understand these guiding principles, you will have a solid foundation on which to build a complete set of
accounting skills. It is useful and necessary that whether an international
company is reporting to its stockholders or a proprietor is presenting information to a bank for a loan, these reports follow a consistent set of rules that
everyone understands and agrees to.

Who Are the SEC, AICPA, and the FASB?
(or What Is This, Alphabet Soup?)

Congress created the Securities and Exchange Commission (SEC) in 1934. At
that time, the Commission was given the legal power to prescribe the
accounting principles and practices that must be followed by the companies
that come within its jurisdiction. Generally speaking, companies come under
SEC regulations when they sell securities to the public, list their securities on
any one of the securities exchanges (New York Stock Exchange or American
Exchange for example), or when they become greater than a specified size as
measured by the firm's Assets and number of shareholders. Thus, since 1934,
the SEC has had the power to determine the official rules of accounting practice that must be followed by almost all companies of any significant size.

Instead, for the most part, the SEC assigned the responsibility of identifying or specifying GAAP to the American Institute of Certified Public
Accountants (AICPA). That role has now been transferred to the Financial
Accounting Standards Board (FASB). All rulings from the FASB are considered to be GAAP. The FASB is currently collaborating on a project with
the International Accounting Standards Board to make it easier for companies to report financial statements, so that separate statements are not needed for U.S. and international markets.

A firm must adopt the accounting practices recommended by the FASB
or the SEC unless they can identify an alternative practice that has "substantial authoritative support." Even when a company can find "substantial

authoritative support" for a practice it uses which differs from the one recommended, the company must include in the financial statement footnotes (or in the auditor's report) a statement indicating that the practices used are not the ones recommended by GAAP. Where practicable, the company must explain how its financial statements would have been different if the company had used Generally Accepted Accounting Principles.

Generally Accepted Accounting Principles (GAAP)

Financial statements must present relevant, reliable, understandable, sufficient, and practicably obtainable information in order to be useful.

Relevant Information

Relevant information is that information which helps financial statement users estimate the value of a firm and/or evaluate how well the firm is being managed. The financial statements must be stated in terms of a monetary unit, since money is our standard means of determining the value of a company.

In the United States, accountants use the stable monetary unit concept, which means that even though the value of the dollar changes over time (due to inflation), the values that appear on the financial statements normally are presented at historical cost. Historical cost presents the information on the financial statements at amounts the individual or company paid for them or agreed to pay back for them at the time of purchase. This method of accounting ignores the effect of inflation. In many other countries throughout the world, the accounting profession does account for inflation.

Alert!

Changes in the Works: As part of the convergence project discussed above, the FASB has started transitioning from the principles of historical cost to fair value. With fair value, the Assets would be shown on the Balance Sheet at what they could be replaced for, or at a value that has been appraised. This normally would be a value higher than the historical cost, or the amount paid for the Asset by the company. Many accountants argue that this value better represents the true value of the Assets on the Balance Sheet.

Not all information about a firm is relevant for estimating its value or evaluating its management. For example, you don't need the information of how many individuals over forty years of age work for the company, or what color the machinery is painted in order to make financial decisions about a company. Even some financial information is not relevant, like how much money the owner of a corporation has in the bank, because as we reviewed in chapter 1, the business's accounting records are kept separate from its owner's, and the owner's financial information is irrelevant to the business.

Reliable Information

Reliable information is key in accounting. Sufficient and objective evidence should be available to indicate that the information presented is valid. In addition, the information must not be biased in favor of one statement user or one group of users to the detriment of other statement users. The need for reliable information has caused the federal government to pass laws requiring public companies to have their records and financial statements examined (audited) by independent auditors who will make sure that what companies report is accurate. This will be the topic of chapter 11.

Verifiable Information

The need for verifiable information does not preclude the use of estimates and approximation. If you were to eliminate from accounting all estimates, the resulting statements would not be useful primarily because the statements would not provide sufficient information. The approximations that are used, however, cannot be "wild guesses." They must be based on sufficient evidence to make the resulting statements a reliable basis for evaluating the firm and its management.

One example of a place in the financial statements where we estimate the value is with depreciation. Once we purchase a Long-Term Asset (anything that the company owns that will last longer than one year; for example, a building), we then need to spread the cost of this building over the life of the Asset. This is called depreciation. In order to do this we must estimate the life of that particular Asset. We can't know exactly how long that will be, but since we do have experience with these types of Assets, we can estimate the Asset's life. We assume that the building will be useable for say twenty years and depreciate (or spread) the cost of the building (the Asset) over twenty years (the estimated life).

For example, if we buy this building for $100,000 and assume that it is going to last twenty years, the annual depreciation would be $5,000 per year ($100,000/20). This $5,000 becomes one of the Expenses for the company and is shown on the Income Statement along with the other Expenses. We will look at this topic indepth in chapter 4.

Understandable Information

To be understandable, the financial information must be comparable. Any item on the Balance Sheet that an accountant labels as an Asset or Liability, users of the financial statements should also call Assets and Liabilities. Statement users must compare financial statements of various firms with one another, and they must compare statements of an individual firm with prior years' statements of that same firm in order to make valid decisions. Thus, the accounting practices that a firm uses for a particular transaction should be the same as other firms use for the identical transaction. This practice should also be the same practice the firm used in previous periods. This concept is called Consistency. Together, information that is comparable and consistent becomes understandable to the users of the financial information.

Quantifiable Information

Information is easier to understand and use if it is quantified. Most information that accountants and users of financial information use is represented by numbers. The information that is presented in the financial statements is presented in a numerical form; however, where that is impossible, the information (if it is relevant, reliable, understandable, and practicably obtainable) will be presented in narrative form, usually in a footnote to the statements. Accountants include narrative information along with the quantifiable information because of the need for adequate or full disclosure; statement users must have sufficient information about a firm.

An example of non-quantifiable information that might be included in the footnotes to the financial statements would be details of an outstanding patent infringement lawsuit against the company, which would be considered a contingent Liability.

Obtainable Information

Furthermore, to be useful, information must be reasonably easy to obtain. This fits into the concept of cost vs. benefit. The information must be worth more than what it will cost to obtain it and must be secured on a timely basis. Financial statements must be prepared at least once a year (in many cases, quarterly or monthly) and attempting to incorporate unobtainable information could seriously delay these schedules.

An example of obtainable information is the number of shares sold by the corporation during the year. Another example would be the amount of sales by the business during the year. An example of information that might not be considered obtainable would be the nitty-gritty details of the pension plan systems used in each of the subsidiaries of a multinational corporation. A more reasonable and easily obtainable piece of data might be the total amount of money that is being spent on the company's pensions around the world.

The Entity Concept

Financial statements must also present information representing each separate entity. (This idea is called the Entity Concept). In other words, the transactions of each business or person are kept separate from those of other organizations or individuals. Therefore, the transactions of the subsidiaries of a multinational corporation must all be kept separate from each other. Even though at the end of the year, the records of all of the subsidiaries might be consolidated into one set of financial statements, the records and transactions of each subsidiary are kept separate during the year.

The Going Concern

It is normally assumed that a company will continue in business into the future. This concept is called the Going Concern Principle. There are several estimates that we make in order to complete the financial statement presentations (for example, depreciation of an Asset over its life), and if we did not assume that the company was going to remain in business in the indefinite future, we could not use this sort of information.

The alternative to the Going Concern Principle is to assume that management plans to liquidate the business. When this is known for sure about a business, a different set of accounting principles and rules are used. In general, when a company liquidates, the Assets of the company will be listed at what they can be sold at rapidly. This amount will usually be below their values stated on the Balance Sheet, since they will be sold at "fire sale" prices.

Realizable Value

Assets normally are not shown on the Balance Sheet at more than either their historical cost or an amount for which they can be sold below historical cost. For example, if a company has Inventory that is listed at a historical cost of $100,000, but due to the economy, the competition, or new technology, is today only worth $8,000, this Asset should be written down and shown on the Balance Sheet at $8,000. The section on conservatism (page 20) sheds more light on this topic. An example of an exception to this rule is with marketable securities (stocks). These Assets are shown on the Balance Sheet at their current market price.

Alert!

Accounting Outside the U.S.: In the United States, for the purpose of preparing financial statements, accountants are not allowed to write up Assets to value higher than the historical cost (defined on page 29). This is not true in all countries of the world, where accountants may argue that if you can write down an Asset to reflect "reality," why not do the same when an Asset increases in value? Thus, in many countries outside of the United States, the accountants are allowed to write up Assets when they increase in value to reflect "market value," as well as write them down when the market value is lower than historical cost. This is an important point to keep in mind when reviewing financial statements prepared in companies domiciled outside of the United States.

Materiality

Financial statements' data must be as simple and concise as possible. An item is considered material when its inclusion or exclusion in the financial statements would change the decision of a statement user. A rule of thumb in accounting might be that any item worth 10 percent of the business' Net Income is considered material and should be reported in financial statements; there is no firm dollar amount to be followed here. The important factor to remember is whether the amount in question will change the user's decision. This concept is called the Materiality Principle.

Items that are not material should not be included on the statements separately. If these items were included in the financial statements they would obscure the important items of interest to the reader. Thus, in some cases, many immaterial items should be grouped together and called "miscellaneous" or the items could be added to other items, so that the total becomes material. That is, the items can be lumped in together with other items that are material and the entire bundle can be considered material.

QUIZ

The owners of a business decide to write up the value of their land, which ten years ago cost $10,000 to purchase and today sits in a prime location of the city and has been appraised at $40,000. Should they value their land on the Balance Sheet at $10,000 or $40,000?

See page 21 for answers.

Conservatism

Another traditional practice that accountants use to guide them in preparing financial statements is called Conservatism. Whenever two or more accounting practices appear to be equally suitable to record the transaction under consideration, the accountant should choose the one that results in the lower or lowest Asset figure on the Balance Sheet and the higher or highest Expense on the Income Statement, so as to not be overly optimistic about financial events. This principle of accounting is highly controversial since while being conservative, we may be violating other generally accepted accounting principles like consistency. In addition, it is often asked, "Why is the lower value better, if the higher value better represents the true value of the Asset?"

An example of the Conservatism Principle in action might be in the presentation of Inventory on the Balance Sheet. There are several different generally accepted accounting methods that are allowed to assign a value to Inventory. The accountant should choose the one that presents Inventory at the lowest value so as not to overstate this particular Asset.

The conservatism idea is misused, however, when the accountant chooses a practice that is not as suitable to the situation as an alternative practice merely to report lower Assets and higher Expenses.

ANSWER

In the United States a company cannot write the value of their Assets above the historical cost of that Asset. The argument is that if they do write the value, it leaves too much room for manipulating the financial statements, which could mislead the users of the financial statements.

The practice of writing up Assets, even though accepted in other foreign countries, would violate such generally accepted accounting principles as: 1) conservatism, 2) reliability, and 3) verifiability.

GLOSSARY

American Institute of Certified Public Accountants (AICPA): The professional organization of the Accounting profession. This group has the responsibility to set the ethics regulations for the profession as well as writing and grading the Certification Public Accountants' Examination (CPA Examination).

Conservatism Principle: Whenever two or more accounting practices appear to be equally suitable to the transaction under consideration, the accountant should always choose the one that results in the lower or lowest Asset figure on the Balance Sheet and the higher or highest Expense on the Income Statement.

Consistency: Practices and methods used for presentation on the financial statements should be the same year to year and process to process. If for any reason the company and their accountants decide to change the method of presentation for any item on the financial statements, they must present a footnote to the financial statements explaining why the methods were changed.

Entity Concept: The principle that requires separation of the transactions of each business or person from those of other organizations or individuals. So for example, when a company is owned by one person, the personal finances of the individual who owns the company are not included on the company's financial statements. The opposite is also true; the financial information of the company is not included in the financial statements of the individual owner.

Financial Accounting Standards Board (FASB): The FASB sets the accounting standards to be followed for the preparation of financial statements. All rulings from the FASB are considered to be GAAP.

Generally Accepted Accounting Principles (GAAP): A standardized set of accounting rules used in the United States and prescribed by various organizations, like the FASB and the SEC. These rules guide the uniform preparation of financial statements.

Going Concern Principle: This principle assumes that a company will continue in business into the future. Without this assumption most of the accounting information could not be presented in the financial statements since we are always making assumptions (e.g., what is the life of a Long-Term Asset). The only way to make this assumption is to further assume that the business will be in existence into the indefinite future.

Historical Cost Principle: According to this rule, most Assets and Liabilities should be represented on the Balance Sheet at the amount that was paid to acquire the Asset, or for the Liabilities, at the amount that was contracted to be paid in the future. No account is taken for either inflation or changing value of Assets over time.

Materiality Principle: This principle states that an item should only be included on the Balance Sheet if it would change any decisions of a statement user. If, for example, a multimillion-dollar corporation were to donate $100 to a charity, this information would not change any decision that management or an owner would make. However, since corporate money was spent, this distribution of the $100 must be combined with other small expenditures and reported as a "miscellaneous Expense."

Obtainable Information: Information reported in financial statements must be accessible in a timely manner without an unreasonable expenditure of resources—for example, time, effort, and money—to be included in the financial statements.

Quantifiable Information: Information is easier to understand and use if it is quantified. However, when the information cannot be quantified but is still relevant to the users of the financial statements, it must be shown in the financial statements in narrative form in the footnotes.

Realizable Value Principle: This indicates that Assets should normally not be shown on the Balance Sheet at a value greater than they can bring to the company if sold. If the original historical cost for example is $5,000, and the maximum that the company can sell that Asset for today is $4,000, this Asset should be shown on the Balance Sheet at the lower amount because of this principle.

Relevant Information: Information reported on financial statements must be relevant in that it helps statement users to estimate the value of a firm and/or evaluate the firm's management. Not all information about a company is relevant to this decision-making process. For example, the number of women versus men currently employed at the company would not be considered relevant, even though it might be important data in other contexts. Thus, this type of information is not included in the financial statements.

Securities and Exchange Commission (SEC): The body created by Congress in 1934. One of its duties is to prescribe the accounting principles and practices that must be followed by the companies that come within its jurisdiction.

Recognition Principle: This is the process of recording Revenue into the financial statements. Revenue is recorded at the point of the transfer of the merchandise or service, and not at the point of receiving the cash. That means, for example, that once a service is provided for which a charge has been incurred, that service should be shown on the financial statements regardless of whether money has actually changed hands. Similarly, Expenses are recognized when incurred, not when the money is exchanged for that particular Expense.

Reliable Information: There should be sufficient and objective evidence available to indicate that the information presented is valid.

Separate Entities: See Entity Concept

Stable-Monetary-Unit Concept: Even though the value of the dollar changes over time (due to inflation), the values that appear on the financial statements in the United States are normally presented at historical cost and do not take inflation into account.

Understandable Information: Financial information must be comparable and consistent. If one accountant calls a particular item an Asset, the accountant must follow the set of rules known as generally accepted accounting principles to arrive at the definition of that Asset. Thus, when any user of the financial statements reads these statements, he understands the meaning and classification of the Asset.

Verifiable Information: Information on the financial statements must be based on sufficient evidence that can be substantiated and provides a reliable basis for evaluating the firm and its management.

Chapter 3

The Balance Sheet and Its Components

Understanding the Balance Sheet

Imagine that you make a list of everything that is important to you. Along with this list you attach values to all of these items. Then you make a list of everything that you owe to others, and again you attach values to these items. Then you subtract the total value of the second list from the total value of the first. Voila! You have just created the basic components of a Balance Sheet.

In a business, the first list of items is called Assets. Assets are valuable resources owned by the business and can be either short- or long-term in nature.

Your second list of items is called Liabilities. Liabilities are what you owe to others for resources that were furnished to the business. The parties to whom the company owes money are normally called creditors. The creditors are said to "have a claim against the Assets." Figure 3.1 illustrates the origin of some Liabilities a company or individual might incur.

Figure 3.1: WHERE DO LIABILITIES COME FROM?

What They Are Called	Where Liabilities Originate
Accounts payable	Purchase of items
Wages payable	Services from employees, not yet paid
Utilities payable	Utilities used, not yet paid for
Notes payable	IOUs
Rent payable	Unpaid rent

Your third list can be labeled Owner's Equity. Owner's Equity reflects the amount the owner has invested in the firm. There are two sources of Owner's Equity:

- The amount of money provided directly by the owner or other investors, called Owner's Investment; and,
- The amount retained from profits, called Retained Earnings.

 **Profit takes many forms:** Profits are not always cash; profit can be made up of promises to pay money as well. For example, when there is a sale for a receivable, there will be Revenue, but no cash coming into the company. The money will come in during a later time period but can be considered profit for the company.

Let's look at an example. The Solana Beach Bicycle Company is a small business that makes, repairs, and sells bicycles. The company was started by Samantha Fernandez in January 2006. Sam (as all of her friends call her) has been an avid bike rider for many years and always felt she could build a "better mouse trap" or bicycle, that is. Sam invested some money she had saved and some that she had inherited into her business.

Take a look at the bicycle company's Balance Sheet in Figure 3.2. This is a proprietorship, because Samantha is the sole owner of the company. The Balance Sheet would look a little different for a corporation. These differences are discussed in chapter 7. (See Appendix B for a real-life example of a Balance Sheet from Station Casinos, Inc.)

Figure 3.2: SOLANA BEACH BICYCLE COMPANY
Balance Sheet
December 31, 2006

Assets

Cash	$17,385
Accounts Receivable	9,175
Allowance for Bad Debts	(175)
Inventory	23,000
Prepaid Insurance	1,000
Truck	8,000
Building	25,000
Land	10,000
Total Assets	$93,385

continued

Liabilities And Owner's Equity	
Liabilities:	
Accounts Payable $3,000	
Mortgage Payable 20,000	
Total Liabilities $23,000	
Owner's Equity:	
Owner's Investment $60,000	
Retained Earnings 10,385	
Total Owner's Equity $70,385	
Total Liabilities & Owner's Equity $93,385	

By looking at the bicycle company's Balance Sheet, you can see that there are several Assets belonging to the company that together are valued at $93,385. You can also see that the company has several Liabilities, valued at $23,000. Finally, when you subtract the Liabilities from the Assets, you can see that the company has equity (also referred to as net worth) of $70,385. This represents a combination of the amount of money that the owner has invested into her business ($60,000), and the profit that was earned and retained in the business since its inception ($10,385). Since this is the first year of business, all of the profit must have been earned this year.

What Does the Date on the Balance Sheet Mean?

There is a great deal of disagreement as to how accountants arrive at the values that are shown above on the Balance Sheet. Of most concern are the values attached to the Assets, and consequently to the Owner's Equity or net worth of the business. The Balance Sheet represents a "snapshot" of the financial position of the business on that specific date. In the case of Solana Beach Bicycle Company, this point in time is December 31, 2006.

The Balance Sheet Is a Snapshot: The numbers that are represented in a Balance Sheet only represent the financial position of the business at the exact point in time for which the Balance Sheet was prepared and no other. In Figure 3.2, this means December 31, 2006, only, not December 30 or January 1. On any other date there might be more or less Assets and Liabilities, and thus the Balance Sheet would look different.

What Is Historical Cost?

As you saw above, all of the items on the Balance Sheet have values attached to them, but where did these numbers come from? In the United States, accountants and other users of financial statements have agreed that financial statements (including Balance Sheets) must be based on historical cost.

This means that the values on the Balance Sheet for Solana Beach Bicycle Company do not represent what the Assets or the Liabilities would be worth today if they were to be sold. Instead, the values represent what was paid for the Assets and what the business agreed to pay to the creditors on the date of the obligation.

Does this confuse the reader of the financial statements? No. Because everyone has agreed to follow this convention, everyone preparing and using these financial statements understands the language that is being spoken.

The Accounting Equation

Often the relationships between Assets (A), Liabilities (L), and Owner's Equity (OE) are shown in terms of a formula.

A = L + OE
Assets = Liabilities + Owner's Equity

The total Assets of the company equal the sum of the Liabilities and the Owner's Equity.

The formula depicts the relationships of the various elements of the Balance Sheet. Balance Sheets are often set up with the Assets on one side (the left side) and the Liabilities and equity on the other (the right side).

The same formula can be stated this way:

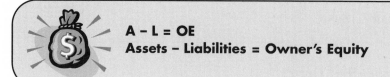

A – L = OE
Assets – Liabilities = Owner's Equity

If you subtract the Liabilities from the Assets, you are left with the Owner's Equity of the business.

The Components of the Balance Sheet

Assets

As was discussed above, Assets are items that are of value and are owned by the entity for which you are accounting. Let's make this idea more specific. For an Asset to be listed on a Balance Sheet of a company, the item must pass three tests.

Figure 3.3: HOW DO WE KNOW WHEN AN ASSET GOES ON THE BALANCE SHEET?

The following items give us some hints.

• The company must control the item. (This usually means ownership.)

• The item must have some value to the company.

• The item must have value that can be measured.

Let's look at some examples. Because of the first test, a traditional Balance Sheet does not list the employees of a company, even though we may refer to them as "Assets" in a non-accounting sense, because the company does control, to a certain extent, but does not own these individuals. But what about basketball players or other professional athletes? Doesn't the team own them? The answer is no. What the team owns is not the players themselves, but the player's contracts. Therefore, in this situation, the basketball team ownership would list the contracts of the players as an Asset.

With the second test almost anything that is used in the business to earn income and to generate cash does have some value. Certain items that do meet the first requirement might be eliminated from being listed as Assets by this test. Examples might include an old truck that does not work or Inventory that cannot be sold any longer because it is now outdated; for example, old versions of computer software.

An example of the third test would be when the company purchases a used machine. The company purchased it for a fixed amount of money and has a record of this transaction that clearly indicates the value of the machine. (Note: Neither the company nor the Balance Sheet deals with an over- or under-paid amount for the machine. The Balance Sheet reflects only historical cost, which is what is recorded as the amount paid for the machine, whether the company paid too much or got a bargain!)

Let's assume that a company has built up a thriving business, and some of the reasons for this growth are the reputation of the owner and the location of the company. Neither the reputation of the owner nor the location of the company has been paid for. We also do not have any way of measuring a value to put onto these items. Therefore, they fail the third test, and cannot be listed as Assets of the business.

Another example of an Asset that would fail the test is any Asset that was given to the company. In this situation, there is no historical cost to the company and thus the Asset would not be reflected on the Balance Sheet, since it does not meet this third test. Now, you might say that we can determine a monetary value for this Asset. And you are right! In many countries, this Asset would then be reflected on the Balance Sheet at that value. However, under generally accepted accounting principles in the United States, since there was no historical cost to this Asset, it would not be listed as one of the company's Assets.

QUIZ

Below is a list of items that might be considered Assets by a company. Indicate whether they should be listed on the Balance Sheet as an Asset and why or why not.

1. A bicycle that belongs to the owner of the company

2. A building used to build and sell the bicycles of the company

3. A broken tool that is not used in the business any longer

4. Employees

5. Money owed to the company from sales of bicycles

6. Money owed by the company to the gas company

7. The land that the company's building is on

8. A truck used to deliver the bicycles to customers

9. Money in the personal bank account of the owner

10. Money paid in advance for a three-year insurance policy on the business

See page 41 for answers.

Short-Term Assets

Assets are normally subdivided on the Balance Sheet into two categories. The first is called Short-Term Assets (or Current Assets). These items will be used or converted into cash within a period of one year or less.

Long-Term Assets

Long-Term Assets (also called Non-Current Assets) are not expected to be converted to cash or totally "used up" in a year or less. Rather, they are expected to be of value to the company for more than a year. Long-Term Assets would include equipment, land, and buildings.

Intangible Assets

Intangible Assets are Assets that cannot be physically touched. They must still meet the three tests mentioned earlier in order to be listed on the

Balance Sheet as an Asset; however, they do not have any tangible characteristics. Some examples of intangible Assets include trademarks, copyrights, and patents, as long as they have been purchased from the prior owner of the business. You might be inclined to call goodwill an intangible Asset; goodwill is based on location of the business, reputation of the owners, and name recognition by the public, and is of great value to a business. Keep in mind, though, that because of the Generally Accepted Accounting Principles discussed in chapter 2, this and any valuable item which was not paid for and thus does not have a historical cost, cannot be listed on the Balance Sheet as an Asset.

Liabilities

Refer to the Balance Sheet of Solana Beach Bicycle Company (fig 3.2). The Total Liabilities of the business are equal to $23,000. As with the Assets, the Liabilities list represents both short-term and long-term items. Again, similar to the list of Assets, the Short-Term Liabilities will be paid off in a period not to exceed one year. The Long-Term Liabilities will remain as debt to the company for longer than one year.

With this or any long-term debt, a portion of it becomes due and payable each year. Thus, most companies' Balance Sheets show the current portion of all long-term debt separately in the Short-Term Liabilities section.

Owner's Equity

As we have discussed above, the equity of Solana Beach Bicycle Company comes from two sources. The Owner's Investment of $60,000 represents the amount invested in the business by the owner through the purchase of various Assets or as money in the bank that is meant for the business. The Retained Earnings of $10,385 represent the amount of profit earned by the business since its inception minus any money that the owner may have taken out for his or her personal use.

Understanding Cash and Retained Earnings: Let's take a moment to clarify a very important point about Retained Earnings that often causes confusion among owners of small and large businesses alike. The Retained Earnings in a business are not equal to cash, that is, "money in the bank." Just because a company has kept profits in the business over the years does not mean that all of these profits have been retained in the form of cash. For example, after the company earns a profit, it may take that cash and purchase Assets or pay off some of its Liabilities. Business owners often assume that they are doing well because they are making profits without taking into account the amount of cash they have at their disposal. If they do not have sufficient cash, however, they will find themselves in dire straits since they may not be able to make the payroll, pay their taxes, or pay for other Liabilities. It is absolutely essential that businesses have a good cash management plan.

A revised Balance Sheet for Solana Beach Bicycle Company using the most common subheadings would look like the one shown in Figure 3.4.

Figure 3.4: THE EXPANDED BALANCE SHEET
SOLANA BEACH BICYCLE COMPANY
Balance Sheet
December 31, 2006

Assets

Short-Term Assets:

Cash	$17,385
Accounts Receivable	9,175
Allowance for Doubtful Accounts	(175)
Inventory	23,000
Prepaid Insurance	1,000
Total Short-Term Assets	$50,385

Long-Term Assets:

Truck	.$8,000
Building	.25,000
Land	.10,000
Total Long-Term Assets	.$43,000
Total Assets	.$93,385

Liabilities and Owner's Equity

Short-Term Liabilities:

Accounts Payable $3,000	
Current Portion of Mortgage Payable 1,000	
Total Short-Term Liabilities	.$4,000

Long-Term Liabilities:

Mortgage Payable	.$19,000
Total Liabilities	.$23,000

Owner's Equity:

Owner's Investment $60,000	
Retained Earnings 10,385	
Total Owner's Equity	.$70,385
Total Liabilities & Owner's Equity	.$93,385

The Transactions Behind the Balance Sheet

Referring to the Balance Sheet in Figure 3.4, let's examine the transactions that created it.

Sam Invests Money in the Company (Owner's Investment)

First, let's assume that on January 1, 2006, Sam invests $60,000 in her bicycle company. In other words, she takes $60,000 out of her personal bank account and sets up a new account with the bank for the new business. After this transaction, the company's Balance Sheet looks like the one presented in Figure 3.5:

Figure 3.5: SOLANA BEACH BICYCLE COMPANY
Balance Sheet
January 1, 2006

Assets	Liabilities & Owner's Equity
Short-Term Assets:	**Liabilities:** $0
Cash $60,000	**Owner's Equity:**
	Owner's Investment . .$60,000
Total Assets $60,000	Total Liabilities and Owner's Equity $60,000

On the Balance Sheet the cash and Owner's Investment are increased by $60,000. Note that the Balance Sheet continues to balance, i.e., Assets = Liabilities + Owner's Equity.

Sam Purchases Land, a Building, and a Truck (Long-Term Assets)

Next, on January 1, the bicycle company buys a piece of land with a building and a truck in order to operate her business. The land has a value of $10,000, the building's value is $25,000, and the truck that will be used for pick-ups and deliveries is $8,000. All of these values are the actual amounts that the company pays. Because the company does not have sufficient cash to pay for all of these Assets at the current time, it decides to borrow some money. It pays $23,000 in cash and takes out a mortgage on the land and building for $20,000 to purchase these Assets. This is a twenty-year loan. One thousand dollars of this loan is due and payable within one year. After these transactions, the company's Balance Sheet looks like the one presented in Figure 3.6:

Figure 3.6: **SOLANA BEACH BICYCLE COMPANY**
Balance Sheet
January 1, 2006

Assets	Liabilities & Owner's Equity
Short-Term Assets:	**Liabilities:**
Cash $37,000	Current Portion of Mortgage Payable . . .$1,000
	Long-Term: Mortgage Payable . . .19,000
Total Short-Term Assets $37,000	Total Liabilities $20,000
Long-Term Assets:	**Owner's Equity:**
Truck $8,000	Owner's Investment . .$60,000
Building 25,000	
Land 10,000	
Total Long-Term Assets $43,000	
Total Assets $80,000	Total Liabilities and Owner's Equity $80,000

As you can see in Figure 3.6 the cash balance has decreased by $23,000 (the amount of cash contributed to the purchase of the land, building, and truck), the other Assets have increased to $43,000 (the truck, building, and land), and two new Liabilities have appeared (the current and long-term portions of the mortgage loan). The loan of $20,000 has been divided up between the short-term portion of $1,000 and the long-term portion (due in a period of greater than one year) of $19,000. Also, notice that the Owner's Equity is not affected.

What are the factors that change Owner's Equity? The items below give us a summary of the *only* items that have an impact on the beginning balance of Owner's Equity.

- The owner invests more money in the business
- The business makes a profit or loss
- The owner takes Assets out of the business.

Thus, when Sam invested the $60,000 into the bicycle company, this increased her Owner's Equity in the company by this same amount. When the company makes a profit, this is also an increase to her Owner's Equity. Finally, if Sam decides to take any money or other Assets out of the bicycle company for her own use, this will reduce the Owner's Equity as it shows up on the bicycle company's Balance Sheet.

Sam Purchases Insurance (Short-Term Asset)

On January 3, the company purchases a three-year insurance policy on the building. The cost of this insurance is $1,500. Because this purchase covers three years and at the time of purchase has not been used up at all, the expenditure represents an Asset. We call this Asset, "Prepaid Insurance." The company pays for this insurance with cash. After this transaction, the Balance Sheet looks like it does in Figure 3.7:

Figure 3.7: SOLANA BEACH BICYCLE COMPANY
Balance Sheet
January 3, 2006

Assets	Liabilities & Owner's Equity
Short-Term Assets:	**Liabilities:**
Cash $35,500	Current Portion of Mortgage Payable . . .$1,000
Prepaid Insurance 1,500	
	Long-Term: Mortgage Payable . .$19,000
Total Short-Term Assets $37,000	Total Liabilities $20,000

Long-Term Assets:		Owner's Equity:	
Truck	$8,000	Owner's Investment	$60,000
Building	25,000		
Land	10,000		
Total Long-Term Assets	$43,000		
		Total Liabilities and	
Total Assets	$80,000	Owner's Equity	$80,000

In Figure 3.7 the only change in the Balance Sheet after the purchase of the insurance is that one Asset (cash) has been exchanged for another Asset (Prepaid Insurance, between Short- and Long-Term Assets) for the exact amount of $1,500.

Sam Orders and Buys Bicycles (Short-Term Assets)

On January 5, Sam orders and buys two different brands of bicycles from two different companies. She buys eighty of one kind that cost $100 apiece, and twenty-five of the other kind that cost her $200 apiece. The total cost of the 105 bicycles to the company is $13,000. This purchase represents a Short-Term Asset known as Inventory.

Inventory is a Short-Term Asset because the company anticipates selling these 105 bicycles in one year or less. As above, with the purchase of the Long-Term Assets, the company does not want to pay for all of these bicycles with cash. It pays $10,000 in cash and agrees to pay the additional $3,000 to the seller at a later date from the sale. This $3,000 becomes an Accounts Payable of the business, and is shown in the Short-Term Liabilities section.

As we saw in Figure 3.1, there are several different types of payables. The term Accounts Payable is reserved for the purchase of Inventory items that are going to be resold by the company.

QUICK Tip

Keeping an Eye on Inventory: Having too little or too much Inventory in a small business will create problems for the company. Drawing up a budget is a critical part of the accounting process that will aid in the planning and control of the company's expenditures and help the business owner to maintain control of all aspects of the business. Budgets will be discussed further in chapter 10.

After this transaction, the Balance Sheet looks like the one in Figure 3.8:

Figure 3.8: SOLANA BEACH BICYCLE COMPANY
Balance Sheet
January 5, 2006

Assets	Liabilities & Owner's Equity
Short-Term Assets:	**Liabilities:**
Cash $25,500	Accounts Payable $3,000
Inventory 13,000	Current Portion of
Prepaid Insurance 1,500	Mortgage Payable 1,000
	Long-term:
	Mortgage Payable . . .19,000
Total Short-Term	
Assets $40,000	Total Liabilities $23,000
Long-Term Assets:	**Owner's Equity:**
Truck $8,000	Owner's Investment . .$60,000
Building 25,000	
Land 10,000	
Total Long-Term	
Assets $43,000	Total Liabilities and
Total Assets $83,000	Owner's Equity $83,000

Once again, the Balance Sheet stays in balance. Assets ($83,000) = Liabilities ($23,000) + Owner's Equity ($60,000).

You'll note that the Balance Sheet in Figure 3.8 dated January 5, 2006, is quite different from the one dated December 31, 2006 in Figure 3.4. This demonstrates how the Balance Sheet can change, representing the company's Assets, Liabilities, and Owner's Equity at any given point in time.

In this chapter, you have learned about the Balance Sheet and the definitions of all of its components. You have learned how these components relate to each other. You have also learned a very important point: Retained Earnings are not necessarily comprised of only cash, and therefore, cash management is a high priority to a business making a profit. Finally, you learned how various transactions affect the Balance Sheet of a small business.

ANSWERS

1. No. This would not appear on the company's Balance Sheet, since this is an Asset that belongs to the owner and not the business.

2. Yes, because this Asset is used by the business.

3. No. This was once an Asset, but is no longer one since it is not used in the operations of the business.

4. No. Although a company's employees are often referred to as "Assets," they are not listed as Assets on a company's Balance Sheet since the company does not own them.

5. Yes. This is called Accounts Receivable.

6. No. This is a Liability, not an Asset (something owed rather than something owned).

7. This depends on whether the company owns the land. If it does, the land is considered an Asset because it has value.

8. Yes.

9. No. This is an Asset of the owner, not of the company, and these Assets are kept separate.

10. Yes, this has future benefit to the company since the insurance company owes them insurance for three years into the future.

GLOSSARY

Accounting Equation: A(ssets) = L(iabilities) + OE (Owner's Equity), The formula depicts the relationships of the various elements of the Balance Sheet to each other.

Accounts Payable: A Short-Term Liability (debt) incurred from the purchase of Inventory.

Assets: Items of value that are owned by the company and are represented on the Balance Sheet. In order for an item to be shown on the Balance Sheet, it must meet three tests: 1) the company must control it or own it, 2) the item must have some value to the company, and 3) this value must be measurable. Assets are categorized as short-term or long-term items.

Balance Sheet: This financial statement is a listing of the Assets (items owned), Liabilities (items owed), and Owner's Equity (what belongs to the owner(s)). The relationships between all these items are represented by the accounting equation.

Creditors: Those individuals or companies to which money or other Assets are owed; for example, the supplier from whom Sam purchased the bicycles and to whom she owes an additional $3,000 is a creditor of the company

Equity: See Owner's Equity

Historical Cost: The amount paid for an item owned by the business (Assets), or the amount incurred in a debt on the date of the agreement to enter into the obligation (Liabilities). Even though over time the values of these Assets and/or Liabilities may change, they will always be shown on the Balance Sheet at their historical cost.

Intangible Assets: Those Assets that are of value to a business and meet all tests of being an Asset, but do not have tangible qualities; for example, trademarks and patents.

Inventory: An Asset held by a business for the purpose of resale. In the case of Solana Beach Bicycle Company, Inventory is the bicycles that the company intends to sell.

Liabilities: Debts owed by a business. They can either be short-term or long-term depending upon when they become due. Short-Term Liabilities are to be paid within a year. Examples in the bicycle company are the Accounts Payable, and the current portion of the Mortgage Payable. Long-Term Liabilities extend beyond one year. An example in the bicycle company is the portion of the mortgage which is due to be paid beyond the current year.

Long-Term Assets: Those items that will be consumed or converted to cash after a period of one year. Examples of these Assets in the bicycle company are the truck, the building, and the land.

Owner's Equity: The difference between what is owned and what is owed; in a company, this amount belongs to the owners. The Owner's Equity is made up of the original and additional investments by the owner, plus any profit that is retained in the business, minus any cash or other Assets that are withdrawn or distributed to the owner(s)

Retained Earnings: The amount of profit earned by the business since its inception, minus any money that is taken out or distributed to the owner(s). At Solana Beach, this is whatever the company earns in selling bikes, minus whatever Expenses are incurred; for example, electricity, gas for the truck, mortgage payments, salaries, etc.

Short-Term Assets: Those Assets that are cash or will be converted to cash or consumed within a period of one year or less. Examples of these Assets in the bicycle company are Cash, Accounts Receivable, bicycle Inventory, and Prepaid Insurance.

Chapter 4

The Income Statement

- Understanding the Income Statement
- The Income Statement Illustrated
- Transactions That Effect the Income Statement

At this point, we are familiar with the Balance Sheet and how it is helpful in showing what Assets Solana Beach Bicycle owns and what Liabilities the company owes. We also learned that the difference between these two items is called Owner's Equity and represents what the bicycle company is "worth" at the end of the year. The final thing that we learned was that the Balance Sheet represents these values for one particular point in time and for that point in time only. It can be considered a snapshot of the business.

Now that her business is up and running, Samantha is very interested in knowing, "What is the bottom line? How much money did I make?" For this information Sam should become familiar with the Income Statement.

Understanding the Income Statement

The Income Statement presents a summary of an entity's Revenues (what the company earned from sales of products and services) and Expenses (what was expended to earn this revenue) for a specific period of time, such as a month, a quarter, or a year. This period of time is known as the accounting period. One key difference between the Income Statement and the Balance Sheet is that the Income Statement reflects a period of time rather than a single moment in time as with the Balance Sheet. The Income Statement is also called a Statement of Earnings or a Statement of Operations.

The preparation of the Income Statement serves several purposes. Often, the only reason one uses the Income Statement is to concentrate on the "bottom line" or Net Income (Revenue minus Expenses). The Income Statement can also be useful for analyzing changes in the Revenue data over a period of time, or determining ratios of particular Expenses to Revenue and how these ratios have been changing over certain periods of time. These two topics will be discussed in chapter 8. (See Appendix B for a real-life example of an Income Statement from Station Casinos, Inc.)

The Income Statement Illustrated

In Figure 4.1 we can see all of the bicycle company's Revenue and Expenses for its first year in business. By reviewing these numbers Sam can also see her "bottom line," that is, her company's Net Income for the year.

In general, Income Statements are organized into three sections. The first section shows the Revenues earned from the sale of goods and/or services for the period being reported. In the case of the Solana Beach Bicycle

Company (Figure 4.1) this period is one year. The second section lists the Expenses the business has incurred to earn these Revenues during the period represented by the Income Statement. The third section is the difference between these Revenues and Expenses in which we hope the Revenues outweigh the Expenses, indicating a profit. If the Expenses are greater than the Revenues, this would indicate a loss—not a great thing in a business.

In the example below, the numbers listed inside of parentheses represent subtractions.

Figure 4.1: **SOLANA BEACH BICYCLE COMPANY**
Income Statement
For the Year Ended December 31, 2006

Sales	$35,500	
Cost of Goods Sold	14,200	
Gross Profit		$21,300
Operating Expenses:		
Salaries and Wages	$5,200	
Bicycle Parts	1,625	
Insurance Expense	500	
Bad Debt Expense	175	
Tools Expense	50	
Bank Service Fee	15	
Total Operating Expenses		$7,565
Net Income from Operations		$13,735
Other Revenue and Expenses:		
Repair Revenue		$3,850
Repair Expenses		(1,100)
Interest Expense		(1600)
Net Income Before Taxes		$15,585
Less: Income Taxes		(4,500)
Net Income		$10,385

The Accrual Concept

The Accrual Concept addresses the issue of when Revenue is recognized on the Income Statement. Revenue is recognized when it is earned and Expenses are recognized as they are incurred regardless of when the cash changes hands; this is referred to as accrual basis of accounting. This type of accounting is used by businesses throughout the United States for the presentation of their financial statements. Some small firms and most individuals still use the cash basis of accounting to determine their income and Income Taxes. Under the cash basis of accounting, Revenue is not reported until cash is received, and Expenses are not reported until cash is disbursed.

Cash Basis of Accounting: The reason a small business might use the cash basis of accounting is that it is easier than the accrual system to keep track of the Revenues and Expenses. No assumptions have to be made (for instance, for depreciation), and no accruals have to be made for items such as Accounts Receivable and Accounts Payable. Accounting entries are only made when cash is actually exchanged.

Generally Accepted Accounting Principles require the accrual system of accounting, and thus most financial statements that you will encounter and that are used by investors and bankers will be prepared under the accrual system of accounting. It is for this reason that throughout the remainder of this book, we will use only the accrual basis of accounting for all of our examples.

Revenue

Revenue (or sales) is what the company earned during a particular period of time from the sale of merchandise or from the rendering of services to its customers. Revenue can come from several sources; a firm can generate Revenue from sales, interest, dividends, royalties, or any combination of these. The sum of all of these sources is the total Revenues of a business.

As shown in Figure 4.1, Revenue of $35,500 is from the sale of bicycles. If you look towards the bottom of the Income Statement, you'll see that the bicycle company also earned Revenue from doing repairs ($3,850). This repair Revenue has been separated from the sales Revenue above, because the main business is sales and not repairs.

At this point there has been no discussion of Net Income. Revenue is one component of Net Income, but it is not the whole story. Expenses and other items need to be added to or subtracted from Revenue to arrive at the Net Income figure.

Revenue Versus Cash Flow: It is important to note that Revenue is not equal to cash flow. Revenue can be generated prior to a business receiving cash. In other words, a sale can be made in which only a promise to pay is generated, but cash does not change hands. Even though the cash will not be collected until some point in the future, the Revenue is recognized at the time that the merchandise has been transferred to the buyer, or the services have been performed by the seller. Therefore, it is possible for a company to have a large amount of sales (or Revenue) and still have a cash flow problem, since they have not collected the money yet.

In Figure 4.1, we can see that the $35,500 of sales was generated by collecting cash and promises to pay cash in the future. You cannot tell simply by reading this one number called Sales how much was generated from each of these two sources individually. But you can tell that at the end of the year, there is still $9,175 owed from the sales, meaning that $9,175 is expected but has not been received in cash yet. You know this from the Balance Sheet in Figure 3.2 (Accounts Receivable at December 31, 2006). The reason that you cannot tell in total how much was sold on account during the year is because some of the Accounts Receivable could have been paid off during the year before this Balance Sheet was generated. The $9,175 only reflects how much is still owed to the business on December 31, 2006.

Expenses

Expenses represent the cost of doing business. Examples of Expenses are rent, utilities, bank service fees, tool and equipment Expenses, bad debt Expense, and salaries. In our current example, the Expenses of Solana Beach Bicycle Company fall under the title of Operating Expenses. These are all of the Expenses for the year 2006 that were incurred by the shop in order to generate Revenue in the operation of the business. The total is $7,565. Another Expense that does not appear in the listing of operating Expenses—but is necessary to generate Revenue—is Cost of Goods Sold ($14,200). This Expense is the cost of either the bicycles purchased by the company or the components used to build the bicycles that were sold during 2006.

There is an important distinction to be made between an expenditure and an Expense. An expenditure is the spending of cash. All Expenses are expenditures; however, not all expenditures are Expenses. It sounds confusing, but it's really quite simple. An Expense is an expenditure that generates Revenue. If the expenditure does not immediately generate Revenue, it is not an Expense. Consider the purchase of a building. When the purchase of a building is made it does not immediately produce Revenue. At that point in time the purchase is considered an expenditure. However, over time this building will be used in the production of Revenue, and the building (and other such Long-Term Assets) depreciate or are used up. The depreciation of the building thus becomes an Expense and is matched with those Revenues it helped to generate.

Net Income

Net income represents the difference between Revenues generated during the period and the related Expenses, which generated that Revenue. Prior to calculating Net Income, a company first calculates gross income. The gross income is sales (or total Revenues) minus the cost of those goods that were sold. Gross income does not take operating Expenses into account; Net Income, on the other hand, is the gross income minus all of the operating Expenses, plus or minus other Revenues and Expenses.

Once again note that the term cash is not used. As with Revenue, part of the "bottom line" or Net Income could be made up of cash, but other parts could be made up of promises to receive cash or promises to pay cash in the future.

QUICK Tip

Expand Your Focus: When evaluating your business, you should not solely concentrate on Net Income in the financial statements. This is certainly a useful number (especially if it is compared to previous years' figures), but there are several other important numbers and ratios that ultimately might be important to your decisions. Some of these numbers might include gross income, the trend of salary Expenses (are they going up too fast?), how much cash is on hand at the end of the year, how sales have been increasing, if at all. Outside of the company it is important to pay attention to the competition as well as the economy as a whole. These are just a few examples of why, if you only focus on the Net Income figure, you will lose sight of the whole picture.

In Figure 4.1, the term "Net Income" appears three times. The first time is "Net Income from Operations." This number, $13,735 represents the income earned from selling bicycles, the main product of Solana Beach Bicycle Company. In addition to selling bicycles, the company also did some repairs. These repairs generated Revenue of $3,850 during the year. This Revenue is shown separately because it is not the main business of this shop. Thus, after the other Revenues and Expenses are added to "Net Income from Operations," a new total is derived labeled "Net Income Before Taxes." This number is $15,585. After the taxes are paid on this total we arrive at the "bottom line" or "Net Income after taxes" of $10,385.

Confusing? Maybe a little, but accounting convention requires that we separate out Net Income from the main operations of the business and from other income earned from other types of sales and services. After these two numbers are shown separately on the Income Statement, we have to show what the government is going to take in taxes before we can finally arrive at the "bottom line."

Interest and Income Taxes

Other items subtracted from Revenues and Expenses before determining the total Net Income are Interest and Income Taxes. Most accountants classify interest and taxes as an "Other Expense" of the period, not as an operating

Expense. The reason for this is that interest and taxes do not produce main-stream Revenue but are necessary to pay in order to stay in business.

Bad Debt Expense

One operating Expense shown in Figure 4.1 is Bad Debt Expense for $175. This Expense represents the amount of the Accounts Receivable that the company anticipates that it will be not be able to collect. Most businesses try to keep this number to a minimum, in order to keep their Expenses low. The amount of $175, in the case of the Solana Beach Bicycle Company is an estimation made by management; in most businesses this estimate is made based upon prior year's experience of their collections of Accounts Receivable.

QUICK Tip

Keep Bad Debts in Check: In order to keep your Bad Debt Expense to a minimum, it is important that you do extensive credit checks on those customers to whom you are going to extend credit. This can be done with the help of professional services such as Dunn and Bradstreet and by reviewing and understanding their financial statements prior to extending this credit.

QUIZ

Based upon your knowledge of accounting so far, looking at the Income Statement in Figure 4.1, would you say that the Solana Beach Bicycle Company had a good first year of business? What would you like to see them do differently next year? What additional information do you need to make these decisions?

See page 60 for answers.

Transactions That Effect the Income Statement

Let's examine the transactions that created the Income Statement in Figure 4.1.

Sales

In the Revenue section above we looked at the total Revenue (or sales) for the year. Now let's look at an individual sale during the year, and see what effect it has on the Income Statement. What we have been looking at in Figure 4.1 is the Income Statement at the end of the year. Now let's go back to the beginning of the year and see how these final figures in Figure 4.1 were arrived at.

Assume that on January 6, the company makes its first sales—two bicycles—for a total of $500. The company originally bought the bikes for $100 each (a total of $200). After this transaction the Income Statement would look like the one in Figure 4.2. (Note that this Income Statement in Figure 4.2 is as of January 6, whereas the one in Figure 4.1, is as of December 31.)

Figure 4.2: SOLANA BEACH BICYCLE COMPANY
Income Statement
For the Week Ended January 6, 2006

Sales	$500
Cost of Goods Sold	200
Gross Profit	$300
Expenses	—
Net Income	$300

This transaction has caused two changes to the Income Statement. First, it has increased the Revenue account called "Sales" by $500, and second, it has increased an Expense account called "Cost of Goods Sold" by the cost of the two bicycles or $200.

At the same time this transaction has changed the Balance Sheet in several ways. Assuming that these bicycles were sold for cash, the Asset account (cash) on the Balance Sheet would increase by $500. A second Asset account called Inventory, where these bicycles were listed when they were bought, would be decreased by the cost of the two bicycles, $200.

The other change on the Balance Sheet is that the Retained Earnings figure goes up by the difference between the sales price of these two bicycles and the cost. Thus, Retained Earnings increases by $300 ($500–$200), the profit made through the sale of the bicycles.

(Note: Remember that Revenue minus Expenses equals Net Income, and Net Income increases Retained Earnings on the Balance Sheet. Once again, a very important part of this concept is that there is no mention of cash. Whether these bikes were sold for cash or the promise to pay cash in the future, is of no importance to the "bottom line" although it is a very important concern from a cash flow management standpoint.)

Now let's look at the Accounting Equation, A = L + OE that we learned about in chapter 1. One Asset, cash, has increased by the sale price of $500. Another Asset, Inventory, has decreased by the cost of the bicycles that were sold, $200. Retained Earnings, part of Owner's Equity, has increased by the difference between the sale price and the cost, or $300. Thus the left side of this equation has increased by $300 (one Asset up $500 and the other down by $200), and the right side of the equation, Owner's Equity, has increased by the same amount, the Net Income of $300.

Using the equation, the transaction would look like this:

Assets = Liabilities + Owner's Equity
Cash + $500
Inventory – $200 = Net Income + $300

This concept is further demonstrated in chapter 6, "Double-Entry Accounting System."

Cost of Goods Sold and Gross Profit

During the complete year of 2006, the cost of the all of the bicycles sold was equal to $14,200. The difference between the sales price of the bicycles ($35,500) and the cost of these bicycles ($14,200) is called the Gross Profit. The word "gross" is used since it represents the profit of the bicycle company *before* the operating Expenses are subtracted. In the case of the bicycle company, the Gross Profit is equal to $21,300.

Operating Expenses

Operating Expenses are those costs that are necessary to operate the business on a day-to-day basis. On January 7, Solana Beach Bicycle Company pays the owner her first week's pay of $100.

Alert!

Paying the Owner: Remember that the owner of this company and the Solana Beach Bicycle Company are two separate entities and when the business pays the owner her salary, this constitutes one entity paying another.

After this second transaction, the Income Statement looks like the one in Figure 4.3:

Figure 4.3: **SOLANA BEACH BICYCLE COMPANY**
Income Statement
For the Week Ended January 7, 2006

Sales	$500
Cost of Goods Sold	200
Gross Profit	$300
Expenses	100
Net Income	$200

The $100 paid to the owner is an Expense (Salary Expense) and as such it is shown in the Income Statement under Expenses. The Net Income is decreased by the entire $100, as is the Retained Earnings and the cash in the Balance Sheet. Assuming that the salary is paid in cash, the impact on the accounting equation would look like this:

Assets = Liabilities + Owner's Equity
Cash − $100 = Net Income − $100

Business Transactions

Selling Bicycles but Receiving Only Partial Payment

On January 21, the bicycle company sold ten more bicycles for a total of $5,000. The cost of these ten bicycles was $2,000. The buyers of these bicycles paid a total of $3,500 in cash and promised to pay the other $1,500 within sixty days.

After this transaction the Income Statement would look like the one below in Figure 4.4:

Figure 4.4: **SOLANA BEACH BICYCLE COMPANY**
Income Statement
For the Week Ended January 21, 2006

Sales	.$5,500
Cost of Goods Sold	.2,200
Gross Profit	.$3,300
Expenses	. . .100
Net Income	.$3,200

Notice that on the Income Statement under the accrual system of accounting, income—like Revenue—is determined when it is earned and has nothing to do with when the cash is received. The entire $5,000 was added to the existing $500 in sales even though only $3,500 cash was received for the ten bicycles. This step is taken because a transaction has occurred in which the buyers have obligated themselves to pay the full $5,000.

The cost of the goods sold (which is an Expense) increased $2,000 because the ten bicycles that were sold had cost the business this amount of money (ten bicycles at $200 each). If we were looking at the Balance Sheet, the Inventory Asset would be decreased by this $2,000, the cost of the Inventory that was sold.

Also, on the Balance Sheet, the Retained Earnings increased $3,000. (Revenue of $5,000 minus Expenses of $2,000.) Now you can see that because of the relationship between Net Income on the Income Statement and Retained Earnings on the Balance Sheet, any time Net Income is changed, Retained Earnings is also changed by the same amount.

So the impact on the accounting equation of $A = L + OE$ would look like this:

Assets	= Liabilities + Owner's Equity
Cash + $3,500	
Inventory – $2,000	= Net Income +,$3,000
Accounts Receivable + $1,500	

Repairing Bicycles and Receiving Cash

On February 14, five customers pick up bicycles they had brought into the shop for repair. The customers paid a total of $375 for the repair of these five bicycles. The cost of the parts to repair these bicycles was $105.

After this transaction the Income Statement would look like the one in Figure 4.5:

Figure 4.5: **SOLANA BEACH BICYCLE COMPANY**
Income Statement
For the Two Weeks Ended February 14, 2006

Sales	$5,500
Cost of Goods Sold	2,200
Gross Profit	$3,300
Expenses	100
Net Income from Operations	$3,200

Other Revenue:

Repair Revenue	$375
Repair Expenses	(105)
Net Income	$3,470

This transaction of repairing the bicycles increased Net Income, cash, and Retained Earnings by $270. Also, the total Assets owned by the company increased by $270.

At this point you should assume that the bicycle parts were bought for cash immediately prior to being used to repair the bicycles. Therefore, there is no Inventory of bicycle parts.

Once again, let's look at the impact on the Accounting Equation:

Assets = Liabilities + Owner's Equity
Cash +$375 (from customers) = Net Income +$270
Cash –$105 (to buy parts)

Other Operating Expenses

During the year, Solana Beach Bicycle Company incurred other Expenses that were necessary to operate the business. The business had to pay interest on the mortgage that it held. Since the mortgage is for $20,000, and the interest rate on this loan is 10 percent, the total interest paid during the year is $2,000. In addition to the interest, the company bought some small tools to use on the repairs, which cost a total of $1,625. The company was also charged a service fee of $15 by the bank where it has its account. The total of these operating Expenses increased the Expenses on the Income Statement and reduced cash and Retained Earnings on the Balance Sheet.

At the end of the year, the owner concluded from prior experiences with business receivables that she was not going to be able to collect $175 from one of the customers that had promised to pay. In order to recognize this on the financial statements, she created an Expense category called Bad Debts Expense. This Expense is increased by the amount of the receivable that will not be collected, and a new account is set up, called Allowance for Doubtful Accounts for the other side of the transaction. This allowance account is called a "contra-Asset" account, and is used to reduce Accounts Receivable on the Balance Sheet.

The last Expense that is listed on the Income Statement, Insurance Expense is another Expense that reduces Net Income without using cash at the time the Expense is recognized. Remember from chapter 3, Prepaid Insurance is listed on the Balance Sheet as an Asset of $1,500. (Refer to page 40 in chapter 3, if you don't remember!) This came about because the bicycle company bought the insurance in advance of using it. Since this was a three-year policy, by the end of year one, one-third of it had been used by the business. To recognize the "using up" of this Asset (Prepaid Insurance), the Insurance Expense is increased by $500 which corresponds to the Expense of using the insurance for one year. Even though the insurance was paid for last year, it is being used one-third at a time during each of the three years. Each time we use the insurance, it represents an Expense to the company even though the cash was expended (an expenditure) in a prior year. Once again, we see the difference between an expenditure and an Expense. We also see that expenditures eventually become Expenses. In year one when the insurance was purchased, it was an expenditure of cash to the company. It does not become an Expense until the insurance policy is actually used for one year.

The Asset itself is no longer worth the full amount paid, since it now only represents the remaining two years. Therefore, the Asset is reduced by the same one-third (one year of the three years), or by $500.

Looking at the impact this would have on the accounting equation, we note the following:

Assets = Liabilities + Owner's Equity
Prepaid Insurance − $500 = Net Income (Interest Expense) − $500

In this chapter you learned the components of an Income Statement and how they relate to each other. You also learned that Revenue and Net Income are not the same as cash because accountants usually use the accrual basis of accounting and not the cash basis. Finally, you learned how individual transactions affect and change the Income Statement.

In chapter 5 you will find out how to prepare and use a Statement of Cash Flows.

ANSWER

It is not possible to make a complete analysis of a company just by looking at one financial statement. Sam, the owner, and we as outsiders would also need to look at the Balance Sheet as well as the Statement of Cash Flows (to be discussed in the next chapter).

It is important to note that the Solana Beach Bicycle Company did make a profit of $10,385. Many new small businesses do not make a profit for the first three or four years, so that is impressive.

In planning for the year ahead, Sam might decide to put more money into advertising and expand the repair business. Only 10 percent of the company's Revenue came from repairs, so there could be room for growth in that area of the business.

Other information that would be helpful to look at includes the other financial statements as well as the budgets for the next two years, 2007 and 2008.

GLOSSARY

Accounts Receivable: This is a term used to describe money that is to be received in the future for current sales of goods or services. Normally, Accounts Receivable appears on the Balance Sheet as a Short-Term Asset since companies generally give credit to customers for thirty to sixty days.

Accrual Basis of Accounting: This accounting method recognizes transactions when Revenue is earned, Expenses are incurred, and purchases take place—whether or not cash changes hands at that moment. This is the method of accounting used by virtue of Generally Accepted Accounting Principle, and most businesses use this rather than the alternative, the cash basis of accounting.

Bad Debt Expense: This Expense appears on the Income Statement and is increased by the amount of the receivables that will not be collected (that is, debts owed to the company that will not be paid). When this Expense is created, a contra-Asset to Accounts receivable is also created called Allowance for Bad Debts. This contra-Asset reduces the Accounts Receivable account on the Balance Sheet and keeps the two sides of the Balance Sheet in balance.

Bottom Line: Another term used for Net Income, it represents all Expenses subtracted from all Revenues. This figure gets it name from the fact that it appears at the bottom of the Income Statement.

Cash Basis of Accounting: This accounting method only recognizes Revenue and Expenses when cash is exchanged. If the sale or Expense takes place in one period without cash changing hands, because of receivables and payables, the Revenue and the Expenses are not recognized until a future period. For this reason, the cash basis of accounting is typically not used for business according to GAAP, but is the method generally used in personal accounting.

Cost of Goods Sold: The cost of all the Inventory that was sold during the period stated in the Income Statement. Cost of goods sold is an Expense and is subtracted from Revenue to arrive at Gross Profit.

Expenditures: The spending of cash. All Expenses are expenditures; however, all expenditures are not Expenses. Only expenditures that immediately generate Revenue are considered Expenses. When expenditures are made for items that have future benefits, they are classified as Assets and converted to Expenses as they are used up.

Expenses: Expenses are expenditures made to generate Revenue. Whether or not cash changes hands, a company incurs an Expense as soon as it makes a commitment to pay for a product or service.

Gross Profit: The difference between Revenue and Cost of Goods Sold before operating Expenses, interest, and taxes are subtracted. A good analysis for the owner of a company is to compare Gross Profit from one year to another and determine whether it is increasing or decreasing and why.

Income Statement: This financial statement is a listing of all Revenues and Expenses of the business earned or incurred during a particular period of time. The Income Statement is usually produced by a company monthly, quarterly, or annually. It is one of the three major statements produced by businesses in the United States, the other two being the Balance Sheet and the Statement of Cash Flows.

Net Income: The difference between Revenue and Expenses for a designated period of time. In the case of Solana Beach Bicycle Company, we saw three uses of the term Net Income. The first, Net Income from operations, shows all normal Revenue and Expenses that deal with the main operations of this business—selling bicycles. The second usage was Net Income before taxes, where Net Income from operations is increased and reduced by other Revenue and Expenses that are outside the normal operations of this business—like repairing bicycles. The third usage was Net Income. This is what is referred to as the "bottom line" since it appears at the bottom of the Income Statement. It is derived by reducing Net Income before taxes, by the amount of Income Taxes for the year.

Other Revenues and Expenses: Those items that are derived from transactions that are not the main business of the company and that are listed on the Income Statement under "Other Revenues and Expenses." In the case of Solana Beach, sales of bicycles is the main business; repairs are not the shop's main business and are listed under "Other Revenues and Expenses."

Recognize: This term refers to the recording of the Revenues and Expenses in the records of the company. This occurs at the point in time when Revenue and Expenses are shown on the Income Statement. Revenues are recognized when services are performed or when title is transferred on goods sold. Expenses are recognized when they are incurred and become an obligation of the company.

Revenue: The amount earned by a business by selling goods or performing services is termed "Revenue." In the case of the Solana Beach Bicycle Company, Revenue represents the earnings in from the selling of bicycles as well as the repair of bicycles. Since the main business of the company is to sell bicycles, the Revenue that is earned from the repairs is shown as other income.

Chapter 5

Preparing and Using a Statement of Cash Flows

After analyzing the Balance Sheet and the Income Statement for Solana Beach Bicycle Company, Samantha had a clear understanding of what her business owned and what she owed, as well as what its "bottom line" is for the year. Although things are looking good so far, Sam has a nagging concern, which she raises at a meeting with her business advisor: "I have read that many small businesses go bankrupt, not because they don't have a great product or a great service, but because they run out of cash. Is that right?"

Well, Sam is right. As we discussed in chapter 4, making a profit, or having a large amount in Retained Earnings, does not equal having cash. And if there is no cash, there is no way to pay the salaries, pay the IRS, or pay any other bills for that matter. In this chapter we will discuss the Statement of Cash Flows and the financial statement, which will help Sam in her quest to stay on top of the cash flow in her business.

What Is a Statement of Cash Flows?

For a company's financial statement to be in accordance with Generally Accepted Accounting Principles (GAAP), the Statement of Cash Flows must be included as one of the four required financial statements. Do you remember the other three? They are the Balance Sheet, the Income Statement, and Statement of Retained Earnings.

The Statement of Cash Flows shows the flow of cash within the business—where the cash came from and how it was spent during the period of reporting (which is generally a month, a quarter, or a year). It also shows the cash flows of the company, divided into categories according to three major activities: operating, investing, and financing. This is helpful to statement users, business owners, investors, and creditors because it indicates the type of transaction that gave rise to each one of the cash flows.

Additionally, the Statement of Cash Flows differs from the Balance Sheet and Income Statement in two key ways. The Balance Sheet shows the financial status of a company at the end of the reporting period (a snapshot), but both the Income Statement and the Statement of Cash Flows show the flow of activity during the reporting period (a short movie compared to the snapshot that is the Balance Sheet). The second difference is that the Income Statement reports this activity on the accrual basis, and the Statement of Cash Flows reports it on the cash basis. Remember from chapter 4, that under the cash basis of accounting, Revenue is not reported until cash is received, and Expenses are not reported until cash is disbursed.

What Is the Purpose of the Statement?

Like the other required financial statements you have learned about—the Balance Sheet and the Income Statement—the Statement of Cash Flows enables users to make decisions about the company. The Statement of Cash Flows is more like the Income Statement than the Balance Sheet in that it is a change statement. It shows the transactions that caused cash levels to change from the beginning of the period to the end. As was mentioned earlier, a company can make a profit or earn a large amount of Revenue but not have enough cash to pay its bills. The Revenue, thus the Net Income, may have been generated (wholly or in part) by promises to pay in the future (Accounts Receivable), so it is critically important to review both the "bottom line" as well as the company's position in cash to really forecast its future.

There are several ways in which you might use a Statement of Cash Flows in your own life. Will you have sufficient cash at the end of the month to purchase additional Inventory? Will you have the cash flow in the future to buy the new equipment you'll need to handle all the growth you're experiencing? Will you have the cash necessary to purchase a new building for the planned expansion? (See Appendix B for a real-life example of a Financial Statement from Station Casinos, Inc.)

Cash and Cash Equivalents

In business the term "cash" has a broader meaning than the amount of cash in the bank at the end of the year. It is also defined as liquid short-term investments; liquid investments are those that can quickly be converted into cash within a very short period of time, usually by cashing them in (in the case of certificates of deposit, for example) or by selling them. For this reason, they are also referred to as cash equivalents. (See Figure 5.1 for examples.) Therefore, whenever the term "cash" is used in this chapter it refers to cash and all cash equivalents.

Figure 5.1: EXAMPLES OF CASH EQUIVALENTS

- Cash in the bank
- Commercial paper (a form of short-term loan)
- Any investment that has a maturity date of less than three months
- Certificates of deposit
- Money market accounts
- U.S. Government treasury bills

The Statement of Cash Flows Illustrated

By looking at the Balance Sheet in chapter 3, Figure 3.2, you can see how much cash the Solana Beach Bicycle Company has at the end of the 2006—$17,385. By reviewing the Statement of Cash Flows in Figure 5.2, we can see where the cash came from and where it went during 2006.

Figure 5.2: SOLANA BEACH BICYCLE COMPANY
Statement of Cash Flows
Year Ended December 31, 2006

Note: Parentheses indicate decreases in cash

Cash Flow from Operating Activities:

Net Income	$10,385
Increase in Accounts Receivable	(9,000)
Increase in Inventory	(23,000)
Increase in Prepaid Insurance	(1,000)
Increase in Accounts Payable	3,000
Total Cash Flow from Operations	($19,615)

Cash Flow from Investing Activities:

Purchase of Truck ....($8,000)

Purchase of Building ....(25,000)

Purchase of Land ....(10,000)

Total Cash Flow from Investing Activities ....($43,000)

Cash Flow from Financing Activities:

Borrowing for the Mortgage $20,000

Owner's Investment 60,000

Total Cash Flow from Financing Activities $80,000

Net Increase in Cash and Cash Equivalents $17,385

(Notice that this is the same number for ending cash on the Balance Sheet in Figure 3.2, since there was no beginning balance in cash, $0 + this change = $17,385)

Now let's examine each of the statement's sections closely.

Operating Activities

As was mentioned earlier, the Statement of Cash Flows reports cash flow related to three areas—operating activities, financial activities, and investment activities. This is because a list of cash flows means more to business owners, investors, and creditors as they analyze the business if they can determine the type of transaction that gave rise to each one of the cash flows.

The operations section of the cash flow statement shows how much cash was generated from operations; that is, the day-to-day running of the business. In the case of Solana Beach Bicycle Company, the cash generated from operations would include the money brought in due to bicycle sales and repairs. This statement always begins with Net Income, the figure calculated on the Income Statement (Revenue minus Expenses). Then the items from operations that cause cash to increase or decrease are added and subtracted.

Since not all of the bicycle company's sales (Revenue) were cash customers, you must subtract the sales on credit (Accounts Receivable) from Net Income to determine the amount of cash generated from these sales. We know from the Income Statement in Figure 4.1 that $35,500 in Revenue from sales was generated in 2006. In Figure 5.2 we can see that Accounts Receivable has increased from a beginning balance (the amount of money the bike shop had at the beginning of the year) of $0 to an ending balance of $9,000. This is the net increase in Accounts Receivable, the receivable minus the allowance for doubtful accounts. This means that of all the sales for the year ($35,500), cash has not been received for $9,000 of that total.

Inventory also has increased from a beginning balance of $0 to $23,000 at the end of the year. This change indicates an increase in one Asset, Inventory, and a decrease in cash because cash was used to purchase that Inventory. Because the Inventory purchase used cash (later you will adjust for the portion that was purchased on account), you must subtract the increase in Inventory in order to determine the cash generated from operations. The reduction to Net Income in our example is $23,000.

Prepaid Insurance represents the cash purchase of insurance that is going to be used in the future. In this example, Solana Beach Bicycle Company has paid $1,500 in cash for this Asset. Since this policy is for three years, at the end of 2006, one-third of the Asset has been used up. The remaining Asset of Prepaid Insurance covers the next two years. The $500 that represents the insurance coverage for 2006, is shown on the Income Statement as an operating Expense, and correspondingly has reduced the Asset Prepaid Insurance. The remaining balance in the Prepaid Insurance account of $1,000 represents an outflow of cash that is not included on the Income Statement. For this reason it needs to be subtracted from Net Income in the operating activities section.

(You may be confused as to why in the case of Inventory, the entire amount of the Asset was deducted in the cash flow statement, but in the case of insurance, only a portion was subtracted. The difference between Inventory and this insurance is the fact that the Inventory was all sold and needed to be adjusted for the full amount. With the insurance only one-third has been used up, and thus only one-third needs to be adjusted in the statement.)

The balance in the Accounts Payable account has increased from the beginning of the year when it was $0 to an ending balance of $3,000. This account represents the purchase of Inventory (bicycles) on account. Towards the top of the statement, we subtracted $23,000 from Net Income for the purchase of Inventory, but since only $20,000 of that was paid with cash and the remaining $3,000 is still owed to the creditor (what we call Accounts Payable), we add that $3,000 back in. In our example this is the reason for the $3,000 adjustment.

When all of these adjustments are made to Net Income, the total represents the cash flow from operations. In this example, there is a negative cash flow from operations of $19,615. What it means in the case of the bicycle company (as can been seen in Figure 5.2) is that instead of receiving all cash for its sales, the Solana Beach Bicycle Company allowed some people to pay later ($9,000 in Accounts Receivable). In addition, Sam took some of the money ($23,000) that came in to buy more Inventory and also purchased insurance, which further reduced the cash balance but did not reduce Net Income. Finally, $3,000 was borrowed in the form of an Accounts Payable that allowed the company to buy part of the Inventory without reducing the cash balance. This transaction does not affect Net Income. It is important to note that having a negative cash flow is not necessarily a bad thing; in this case it is acceptable because the company is expecting to receive cash within a relatively short period from Accounts Receivable. If, however, the company were to operate at a negative cash flow for an extended period, it could put its levels of available cash and its ability to settle its own debts in jeopardy.

Investing Activities

Any time a company makes a purchase of property, plant, or equipment, this addition is treated as an investment in the organization. This investment represents a cash flow from the company. Even though the entire purchase may not have been with cash, but with some borrowed money, the entire purchase is shown as a cash flow in the investing section of the cash flow statement, and any borrowing of money is shown separately in the financing section.

In Figure 5.2 we can see that the Solana Beach Bicycle Company purchased three Long-Term Assets during the year 2006. The land for $10,000, the building for $25,000, and the truck for $8,000 are all shown as negative cash flows in the investing activities section of the cash flow statement. The total of these three purchases represents a negative cash flow from investing activities of $43,000.

Financing Activities

The section called financing activities represents the cash that has come into or out of the company for the purpose of financing all of the other activities of the business. This could include Retained Earnings and money brought in by stock issued by the company, or as we can see in Figure 5.2 the $60,000 that Samantha invested into the business on the first day. (Remember that Sam's personal money is accounted for separately from the company's money. If she invests personal funds in the business, while this is a decrease in her personal cash funds, it is an increase in funds for the business.) Because this investment was in cash it is shown as an increase in the cash flow from financing activities. In addition to this investment by Sam, a fifteen-year loan was negotiated in order to purchase the land and the building. This loan for $20,000 is also shown as an inflow of cash to the business and thus an increase in cash flow from financing activities.

The total of these two items, $80,000, represents the total cash flow into the company from financing activities during the year 2006.

The total of the three cash flows—from operations, from investing, and from financing—represents the total increase or decrease in cash and cash equivalents for the business during the year being reported (in this example, an increase of $17,385). Notice that this total represents the change in cash from the beginning of the year to the end of the year. In our example, cash at the beginning of the year was $0, and at the end was $17,385, a net increase.

In this chapter you have learned how to prepare the Statement of Cash Flows. In chapter 6 you will learn about the double-entry system of accounting and how transactions are recorded in the accounting books.

GLOSSARY

Statement of Cash Flows: One of the four required financial statements. This statement shows where the cash came from and how it was spent during the period of reporting.

Cash: Includes currency and coins, balances in checking accounts as well as any item that is acceptable into these checking accounts, such as checks and money orders.

Cash Equivalents: The cash held by a business as well as the liquid short-term investments that can quickly be converted into cash within a very short period of time.

Operating Activities: One of the three categories of business activity represented on the Cash Flow Statement. This section of the statement shows how much cash was generated from operations; that is, the day-to-day running of the business. In the case of Solana Beach Bicycle, this would include cash generated from bicycle sales and repairs.

Investing Activities: One of the three categories of business activity represented on the Cash Flow Statement. This section of the statement shows those purchases of property, plant, or equipment. These items are treated as an investment in the organization and represent a cash flow out of the company.

Financing Activities: One of the three categories of business activity represented on the Cash Flow Statement. This section of the statement represents the cash that has come into or out of the company for the purpose of financing all of the other activities. In the case of Solana Beach Bicycle Company this includes the money borrowed on the mortgage and the money invested in the business by Sam.

Chapter 6

Double-Entry Accounting

- ▶ The General Journal
- ▶ The General Ledger
- ▶ Adjusting Journal Entries
- ▶ Closing Journal Entries

The terms "debit" and "credit" are enough to induce fear in even the most intrepid non-accountant. But even though you may never become an accountant, you will need to understand these concepts in order to have a solid grasp of accounting and business. In this chapter you'll learn what these terms mean and how they are used in the world of accounting.

Alert!

What Is a Debit?: The word debit simply refers to the left side of the amount columns and the word credit identifies the right side of the amount columns. Nothing more, nothing less. Debit does not mean something unfavorable and credit does not mean something favorable, as some non-accountants often believe.

The General Journal

Some time after a business transaction occurs it is recorded in a book called the general journal. While there are many different kinds of journals, it is most important to focus on the general journal. A general journal is often referred to as the book of original entry because this journal is the book in which a transaction is first recorded.

If a company were to buy land for cash, the pages of a general journal will look like the one shown below in Figure 6.1 (the entries in this figure do not come from Solana Beach Bicycle Company but are simply examples):

Figure 6.1:
JOURNAL

			Amounts	
Date	Entries	Reference	Debits	Credits
01/05/06	Land		$10,000	
	Cash			$10,000
(Bought Land for cash for new warehouse)				
01/31/06	Salary Expense		$400	
	Cash			$400
(Paid Salary for the month of January with cash)				

Journal Entries

To illustrate how transactions are recorded in the general journal you can use the transactions described in chapters 3 and 4. But first let's go back to the Accounting Equation we talked about in chapter 1.

$$A = L + OE$$

The standard accounting rule is that Assets, or the left side of the equation, are increased with debits, and decreased with credits, while the right side of the equation, the Liabilities and the Owner's Equity items are just the opposite; that is, they are increased with credits, and decreased with debits. When you increase or decrease the debits, by the same amount as you increase or decrease the credits on each transaction, you make sure that the debits always equal the credits, a key goal of bookkeeping. If the debits do not equal the credits at the end of the period, (month, quarter, or year), it indicates that a mistake was made somewhere along the line and one of the transactions was entered improperly. By using this system, the Accounting Equation always stays in balance after each transaction is recorded since you are increasing or decreasing both sides of the equation by equal amounts. There is a standard way of dealing with debits and credits assigned to Assets, Liabilities, Owner's Equity, Revenues, and Expenses. Figure 6.2 below summarizes this concept:

Figure 6.2:
INCREASES/DECREASES IN ACCOUNTS

Transaction	Journal Entry
Assets Increase	Debit
Assets Decrease	Credit
Liabilities Increase	Credit
Liabilities Decrease	Debit
Revenue (OE Increases)	Credit
Expense (OE Decreases)	Debit

Now let's record in the general journal some of the transactions of the previous chapters. It is important to remember that every single transaction in the journal must be recorded as both a debit and a credit. First, Sam invested $60,000 in her bicycle company. This transaction would be recorded as shown in Figure 6.3:

Figure 6.3:
JOURNAL

Date	Entries	Reference	Debits	Credits
2006				
Jan 1	Cash		$60,000	
	Owner's Investment			$60,000
	(Owner Invests $60,000 in Cash)			

You already know that whenever the owner of a business invests cash into his or her business, cash is increased and so is the Owner's Investment (part of Owner's Equity). If cash (an Asset) increases, this is shown as a debit in the journal; the increase in Owner's Equity is listed as a credit. (See Figure 6.2 above.)

In the next transaction, the company buys a building, land, and a truck for $43,000. Since the bicycle shop does not have sufficient cash to pay for all of these Assets, the owner needs to borrow $20,000 and pays the remainder in cash ($23,000). This transaction would be recorded in the general journal as shown in Figure 6.4:

Figure 6.4:
JOURNAL

			Amounts	
Date	Entries	Reference	Debits	Credits
2006				
Jan 3	Truck		$8,000	
	Building		$25,000	
	Land		$10,000	
	Cash			$23,000
	Mortgage Payable			$20,000
	(Purchase of Assets for Cash and Mortgage)			

Notice in the above journal entry, DEBITS were used to increase the Assets (land, building, and truck), while CREDITS were used to decrease Asset (cash), but to increase the Liability Mortgage Payable. Thus, depending upon which side of the accounting equation the account appears, this will determine if it is recorded as a debit or a credit (see Figure 6.2).

Now we'll move on to the transactions from chapter 4, which were recorded on the Income Statement.

On January 5, the bicycle company sold two bicycles for a total of $500. As you remember, this one transaction caused two changes to the Income Statement. First, it increased the Revenue account called "Sales" by $500, and second, it increased an Expense account called "Cost of Goods Sold" by the cost of these two bicycles or $200. Remember also that at the same time that this transaction is causing a change to the Income Statement, it is also causing the Balance Sheet to change in several ways. These bicycles were sold for cash; thus, the Asset cash would increase by $500. The Asset Inventory would decrease by their cost of $200 (since the bicycles (Inventory) do not belong to the company any longer). The $300 difference between the sale price and the cost ($500 − $200) would be an increase to Retained Earnings, which is part of Owner's Equity.

Notice in the transaction below in Figure 6.5, there is no entry for Retained Earnings or Owner's Equity. The "profit" from this transaction of $300, simply appears in the Balance Sheet (as Retained Earnings) when the Revenue ($500) and the Expense ($200) are recorded.

These two transactions would be recorded in the general journal as seen below in Figure 6.5:

Figure 6.5:
JOURNAL

Date	Entries	Reference	Debits	Credits
2006				
5 Jan	Cash		$500	
	Sales			$500
Also:				
5 Jan	Cost of Goods Sold		$200	
	Inventory			$200
	(Sold Bicycles)			

Referring back to the Accounting Equation, A = L + OE, the sales transaction has increased the left side (the Asset Cash) by $500, and increased the right side, Owner's Equity by the same amount. The second part of this transaction that reduces the Inventory also keeps the accounting equation in balance, the Expense of the bikes (the debit), and the decrease in Inventory (the credit). In both of these transactions, the debits to record these transactions are equal to the credits.

Looking at another transaction in chapter 4, Operating Expenses, you can see the impact on the General Journal. On January 7, Solana Beach Bicycle Company pays Sam her first week's pay of $100. This transaction would be recorded in the General Journal as shown in Figure 6.6:

Figure 6.6:
JOURNAL

Date	Entries	Reference	Debits	Credits
2006				
7 Jan	Salary Expense		$100	
	Cash			$100
	(Paid Salaries)			

This transaction has decreased the left side of the accounting equation, Assets or Cash by $100, and has also decreased the right side Owner's Equity with an Expense by the same amount. Once again, the debits equal the credits.

Finally look at one more transaction from chapter 4, where Solana Beach Bicycle Company repairs some bicycles for $375. The parts for these repairs cost the company $105, paid for in cash. This transaction is recorded in the General Journal as follows in Figure 6.7:

Figure 6.7:
JOURNAL

			Amounts	
Date	Entries	Reference	Debits	Credits
2006				
14 Feb	Cash		$375	
	Repairs Revenue			$375
Also:				
14 Feb	Repairs Expense		$105	
	Cash			$105
	(Performed Repairs)			

Once again, notice that in the first part of this transaction, the left side of the accounting equation is increased by $375, and the right side, Owner's Equity (via a Revenue item), is increased by the same amount.

In the second part of the transaction, the right side is decreased with a credit to an Asset (cash) by $105, and the left side is decreased with a debit to an Owner's Equity account (Repairs Expense). Thus the equation (A = L + OE) stays in balance, and the debits equal the credits.

The General Ledger

During the month, the journal entries made to record the January transactions would be posted from the general journal to the general ledger. The general ledger is a book containing a record of each account. (See boxed section below Figure 6.8.) Posting is simply the process of transferring the information from the general journal to the individual account pages in the general ledger. The cash account, which probably is the first page (or pages) in the general ledger, would look like the example in Figure 6.8:

Figure 6.8

	CASH					**Account #101**	
Date	Comments	Ref.	Debit Amount	Date	Comments	Ref.	Credit Amount

Notice that the account has two sides. As before, the left side is used to record the debits and the right side is used to record the credits.

Notice that the sample ledger account in Figure 6.8 lists an account number, 101 in the upper right hand corner. Every Asset, Liability, Owner's Equity, Revenue, and Expense item has a number assigned to it. Usually, the Assets are the 100s, the Liabilities the 200s, the Owner's Equity the 300s, the Revenues the 400s, and the Expenses the 500s. In the ledger, each item (or account) has a separate page with a separate number. In this case, cash has been assigned the number 101, and all cash transactions are recorded on this page.

The accounts are usually numbered for a variety of reasons; for example, to facilitate referencing or for use instead of the account name. This listing of accounts is normally called the chart of accounts.

After posting the first journal entry (January 1), the cash account would look like Figure 6.9:

Figure 6.9

	CASH					**Account #101**	
Date	Comments	Ref.	Debit Amount	Date	Comments	Ref.	Credit Amount
Jan 1		J-1	$60,000				

The date of the transaction is entered in the date column on the left-hand side since the entry was a debit. J-1 is entered in the reference column and that tells you that the journal entry that recorded the transaction can be found on page one of the general journal. Sixty-thousand dollars is entered in the left-hand amount column.

The other half to this first journal entry (the credit) would be posted to the Owner's Investment account and would be recorded as shown in Figure 6.10:

Figure 6.10

OWNER'S INVESTMENT							Account #301
Date	Comments	Ref.	Debit Amount	Date	Comments	Ref.	Credit Amount
Jan 1		J-1					$60,000

Of course, in this instance the data is posted to the right-hand column since the entry is a credit to the account.

Now after posting the first entry, the general journal would appear as shown in Figure 6.11:

Figure 6.11: TO RECORD $60,000 INVESTMENT BY OWNER

	JOURNAL		Page 1	
Date	Entries	Ref.	Amounts	
			Debits	Credits
2006				
Jan 1	Cash	101	$60,000	
	Owner's Equity	301		$60,000

You see that the account numbers for the cash and Owner's Investment accounts have now been entered in the reference column of the journal. This step completes the posting process for the first journal entry. The same procedure is repeated until all the journal entries have been posted to the general ledger.

After posting all the journal entries recorded in January, the cash account would look like Figure 6.12:

				Figure 6.12				

Figure 6.12

				Cash			**Account #101**	
Date	Comments	Ref.	Debit Amount	Date	Comments	Ref.	Credit Amount	
Jan 1	Investment	J-1	$60,000	Jan 1	Assets	J-1	$23,000	
				Jan 3	Insurance	J-1	$1,500	
				Jan 5	Inventory	J-1	$10,000	
Jan 6	Sales	J-1	$500	Jan 7	Salary	J-1	$100	
Jan 21	Sales	J-1	$3,500					
	Total		$54,000		Total		$34,600	

If you add the debit and credit sides of the cash account, you will find that the debits total $54,000 and the credits total $34,600. The difference between these two figures is $19,400. You could say that the cash account has a debit balance at the end of January. Remember, in order to increase an Asset, we record a debit. If at the end of the period there is a debit balance in an Asset account, that means that there is a positive balance, or in this case with cash, "money in the bank." Debits and credits will generally not be equal for each individual account; but once all the accounts are considered together, the debits and credits should be equal. This is reflected on the trial balance for the cash account before adjustments. A discussion of the trial balance follows below.

Trial Balance

Typically, accountants and bookkeepers will prepare a trial balance from the general ledger after all transactions have been recorded and posted. A trial balance is merely a list of all accounts in the general ledger that have a balance other than zero, with the balance in each account shown and the debits and credits totaled. A trial balance of Solana Beach Bicycle Company at January 31, 2006, would look like the one below in Figure 6.13:

Figure 6.13: SOLANA BEACH BICYCLE COMPANY

Trial Balance
(Before Adjusting & Closing Entries)
January 31, 2006

	Debits	Credits
Cash	$19,400	
Accounts receivable	1,500	
Inventory	20,800	
Prepaid Insurance	1,500	
Truck	8,000	
Building	25,000	
Land	10,000	
Accounts Payable		$3,000
Mortgage Payable (Long-Term)		20,000
Owner's Investment		60,000
Retained Earnings		-0-
Sales		5,500
Repair Revenue		-0-
Cost of Goods Sold	2,200	
Expenses (Salary)	100	
	$88,500	$88,500

A trial balance is prepared by first turning through the pages of the general ledger and locating each account with a balance other than zero, as in Figure 6.12 where the cash account had a debit balance of $19,400. Once it is determined what the balance in each account is, this is noted on the trial Balance Sheet. Generally speaking, the trial balance is prepared for two reasons: the first reason is to determine whether the total debits equal the total credits. If they do not equal, some kind of error has been made either in the recording of the journal entries or in the posting of the general ledger. In either case, the error must be located and corrected. The second reason is to facilitate the preparation of adjusting entries (discussed in the next section), which are necessary before the financial statements can be prepared.

You should note that if Solana Beach Bicycle Company had been in operation prior to this year, a Retained Earnings figure would appear on the present trial balance. The Retained Earnings account will show the beginning Retained Earnings until the accountant closes the accounts that affect the Retained Earnings by the amount of the profit or loss for the period (month, quarter, or year). For more information on closing accounts, see Closing Journal Entries, page 93.

Adjusting Journal Entries

Accounting records are not kept up to date at all times. To do so would be a waste of time, effort, and money because much of the information is not needed for day-to-day decisions. Adjusting entries is a step taken to recognize financial events that have occurred prior to the financial statements' issuance date but which have not been recorded in the journal. These are not transactions with a particular date attached, but they are financial realities which require documentation in order to maintain accurate records. In the case of the Solana Beach Bicycle Company there are five items that need to be adjusted at the end of each month: Accumulated Depreciation on the building and on the truck, Prepaid Insurance, Interest on the mortgage, and the portion of account receivables that the company does not believe it will ever be able to collect (bad debts). After the adjusted journal entries are recorded in the journal, they must be posted to the accounts in the general ledger, just like the earlier journal entries.

Prepaid Insurance

Remember in chapter 3, Prepaid Insurance is listed on the Balance Sheet as an Asset. This came about because Solana Beach Bicycle Company bought insurance in advance of using it. By the end of January, one thirty-sixth of the three-year policy had been used up and became an Expense. To recognize the "using up" of this Asset (called Prepaid Insurance), an Expense called Insurance Expense is increased by $41.67 ($1,500/36 months). The Asset itself is no longer worth the full amount paid, since it now only represents the remaining thirty-five months. If you think back to the accounting equation again—A = L + OE—the left-hand side of the equation is reduced by $41.67 (because the Asset called Prepaid Insurance has decreased), and the right side is also reduced by the same amount because of insurance Expense (which causes a reduction in Owner's Equity). An adjustment for this amount will be made in the journal.

Depreciation Expense

Long-Term Assets like the building and truck have a finite life. Their original (historical) cost is therefore spread over their useful lives. This process is called depreciation. In order to depreciate these two Assets, you need to know what the life expectancy of each is, that is how long these Assets will produce income for the business. In our example, you can assume that the building has a life expectancy of twenty-five years, and the truck of five years. To depreciate these two Assets, you can divide the historical cost by the life expectancy.

Truck:
$8,000 (historical cost)/5 years (life expectancy) = $1,600 Depreciation
per year

Building:
$25,000 (historical cost)/25 years (life expectancy) = $1,000 Depreciation
per year

Since you are only looking for the depreciation adjustment for these two Assets for the month of January, each number would be divided by twelve (months) to arrive at depreciation adjustment for the month of January.

Truck = $1,600 (depreciation per year)/12 (months per year) = $133.33 per month

Building = $1,000 (depreciation per year)/12 (months per year) = $33.33 per month

---

QUICK Tip

The Life Expectancy of an Asset: One of the assumptions you as the owner of a business need to make is what the life expectancies of Long-Term Assets are. How should you do this? The easiest way is to estimate based on your experience of similar Assets used in the business in the past. You can also get information from the library on what averages are used for similar Assets in your industry. Finally, the IRS has a schedule of Long-Term Assets, with life expectancy figures that they will accept. The final decision is yours, and if reasonable, it is acceptable.

Interest Expense

As you remember, Solana Beach Bicycle Company has to pay interest on the mortgage that it took out on the land and building. The mortgage was for $20,000 for ten years at 8 percent per year. The total interest per year is $1,600 ($20,000 x 8 percent). Therefore, each month the business owes the mortgage company one-twelfth of the year's total interest or $133.33 ($1,600/12 months). Since the cash is not owed until the end of the year, Solana Beach Bicycle Company has created another Liability called Interest Payable that is due at the end of the year. The amount of this Liability is the same as the Interest Expense of $133.33 for the month of January.

Accounts Receivable Write-Offs

At the end of January, the company assumed that it was not going to be able to collect $50 from some of the customers that had promised to pay. (This was a guesstimate or assumption, since the company will not know until next month who is going to pay and who is not.) In order to recognize this assumption on the financial statements, Sam created an Expense category called Bad Debts Expense. The other half of this entry is to increase an account called "Allowance for Doubtful Accounts." This account is called a "contra-Asset"; it is a reduction to Accounts Receivable that factors in the expectation that certain Accounts Receivable will not be paid and keeps the Balance Sheet in balance. You should note that even though the Bad Debt Expense does not use cash, it reduces the Net Income in the same way as other Expenses that do use cash. In the case of Bad Debt Expense, the Asset reduced is Accounts Receivable (rather than cash).

QUICK Tip

Estimating Bad Debts: Like depreciation, the management of the company must estimate bad debts for the period. This estimation can be done based on past experience that a certain percent of receivables cannot be collected. It is also possible that management has specific information on particular accounts that will not be collected and can incorporate this data into the adjustments.

Trial Balance After Adjustments

After the adjusting entries are posted to the journal, the accountant may prepare another trial balance to help in the preparation of the actual financial statements, or the accountant may be able to prepare the statements by using the general ledger only. A trial balance prepared at the end of January 2006 would look like Figure 6.14:

Figure 6.14: SOLANA BEACH BICYCLE COMPANY

Trial Balance
(After Adjustments, Before Closing)
January 31, 2006

	Debits	Credits
Cash	$29,400.00	
Accounts Receivable	1,500.00	
Allowance for Doubtful Accounts	(50.00)	
Inventory	10,800.00	
Prepaid Insurance	1,458.33	
Land	10,000.00	
Building	25,000.00	
Accumulated Depreciation-Building	(33.33)	
Truck	8,000.00	
Accumulated Depreciation-Truck	(133.33)	
Accounts Payable		$3,000.00
Interest Payable		133.33
Mortgage Payable (Long-Term)		20,000.00
Owner's Investment		60,000.00
Retained Earnings		-0-
Sales	5,500.00	
Repair Revenue	-0-	
Cost of Goods Sold	2,200.00	
Salaries Expenses	100.00	
Insurance Expense	41.67	
Depreciation Expense	166.66	
Interest Expense	133.33	
Bad Debt Expense	50.00	
	$88,633.33	$88,633.33

There are some differences between this trial balance and the one on page 86, which shows the trial balance before the adjusting journal entries. First, four new accounts have been created: Insurance Expense, Depreciation Expense, Accumulated Depreciation, and Interest Expense.

The account called Insurance Expense represents the amount of the used up Prepaid Insurance for one month. It was increased by $41.67 at the same time that Prepaid Insurance (the Asset) was decreased by the same amount.

The Depreciation Expense account was created to represent the depreciation on the two Long-Term Assets, truck, and building. Instead of reducing the Long-Term Assets directly as they get older, accountants set up another separate contra-Asset account. This, like the one discussed above for Allowance for Doubtful Accounts, was a reduction to Accounts Receivable. For Long-Term Assets the contra account is called Accumulated Depreciation. Each Long-Term Asset has a separate contra-Asset account. (Accumulated Depreciation-Truck and Accumulated Depreciation-Building.) On the Balance Sheet, the contra-Assets would appear like those shown in Figure 6.15 below:

Figure 6.15: PARTIAL BALANCE SHEET

Current Assets:

Accounts Receivable $1,500

Less: Allowance for Doubtful Accounts . . . .(50)

Net Accounts Receivable $1,450

Long-Term Assets:

Truck $8,000

Less: Accumulated Depreciation—Truck . . . .(133)

Net Truck $7,866.67

Land, even though it is a Long-Term Asset, does not depreciate and does not have an accumulated depreciation contra-Asset account.

The last new account is Interest Expense. This account represents the amount of interest that has been paid. In our example, this is $133.33 per month on the Mortgage.

Closing Journal Entries

In general, accounting records are closed at the end of the year. After the closing journal entries have been made and posted, all the Income Statement accounts (also called temporary accounts) begin the new year with a zero balance. For example, next year we want to accumulate and show in the sales account the total sales made during that year and that year only; to do this, the sales account must have a zero balance at the beginning of the year so the figures from the previous year don't carry over.

When Solana Beach Bicycle Company decides to make the financial statements for the end of the month, the accountant would make the following entries in the general journal as shown in Figure 6.16 to close the records for January, 2006:

Figure 6.16				
JOURNAL			**Page 5**	
Date	Entries	Ref.	Amounts	
			Debits	Credits
2006				
Jan 31	Sales		$5,500.00	
	Cost of Goods Sold			$2,200.00
	Salaries Expense			100.00
	Insurance Expense			41.67
	Depreciation Expense			166.66
	Interest Expense			133.33
	Bad Debt Expense			50.00
	Retained Earnings			2,808.34

Each Revenue and Expense account is closed (brought to a zero balance) by (1) determining the balance of the account and (2) placing this amount (the account balance) on the opposite side of the account; that is, a debit balance for an account is balanced out on the credit side of the journal, and a credit balance is balanced out on the debit side. For example, prior to closing, the sales account had a credit balance of $5,500. To close the sales account it was debited for $5,500 to achieve the desired zero balance. The Cost of Goods Sold account had a debit balance of $2,200; thus, to close this account it was credited for $2,200.

After all of the Revenues and Expenses have been closed (made to have a zero balance), and the debits and credits are added in the journal, there will be a dollar difference. In the example, this difference is the difference between the sales debit and the credits for the various Expenses: $2,808.34. This represents Net Income for the month of January. In order to make the closing entry balance an additional credit is needed; this credit is to Retained Earnings. As you learned in previous lessons, Retained Earnings is the account where profits are accumulated from year to year.

QUICK Tip

Handling Revenue and Expense Accounts: Revenue and Expense accounts are temporary accounts. You can close them any time you want summarized information about their financial position. At the end of the accounting period all Revenue and Expense accounts are closed into the Retained Earnings account. This leaves all of the Revenue and Expense accounts with a zero balance after the closing process and lets the statement reader know how much profit or loss has been created by the business.

Before posting the closing entries, the sales and Cost of Goods Sold accounts (for example) looked like Figure 6.17:

Figure 6.17

Sales   Account #401

Date	Comments	Ref.	Debit Amount	Date	Comments	Ref.	Credit Amount
				2006			
				Jan 6		J-1	500.00
				Jan 21		J-1	5,000.00

Cost of Goods Sold   Account #501

Date	Comments	Ref.	Debit Amount	Date	Comments	Ref.	Credit Amount
2006							
Jan 6		J-1	200.00				
Jan 21		J-3	2,000.00				

After posting the closing entries, the sales and Cost of Goods Sold accounts would look like Figure 6.18:

Figure 6.18

Sales   Account #401

Date	Comments	Ref.	Debit Amount	Date	Comments	Ref.	Credit Amount
				2006			
				Jan 6		J-1	500.00
Jan 31	Closing	J-5	5,500.00	Jan 21		J-1	5,000.00

Cost of Goods Sold   Account #501

Date	Comments	Ref.	Debit Amount	Date	Comments	Ref.	Credit Amount
2006							
Jan 6		J-1	200.00				
Jan 21		J-3	2,000.00	Jan 31	Closing	J-5	2,200.00

Notice that in the trial balance in Figure 6.19, there are no Revenue or Expense accounts listed. However, the difference between the Revenue and Expenses prior to their closing has now been closed and appears in the Retained Earnings account.

The double lines drawn across the accounts in Figure 6.18 are meant to indicate that the accounts are closed. Entries for the following period (in this example, February 2006) would be posted to these accounts in the spaces under the double lines. All of the accounts that were closed would look like the sales and Cost of Goods Sold accounts illustrated above in that the debits and credits would balance, except, of course, the dates and dollars figures would be different.

Often accountants will prepare an after-closing trial balance to see that the debits and credits are still in balance and to see that all the temporary accounts have been closed. Solana Beach Bicycle Company's after-closing trial balance would look like Figure 6.19. Notice that accumulated depreciation is listed as a subtraction on the debit side.

Figure 6.19: SOLANA BEACH BICYCLE COMPANY

Trial Balance
(After Closing)
January 31, 2006

	Debits	Credits
Cash	$29,400.00	
Accounts Receivable	1,500	
Allowance for Doubtful Accounts	(50)	
Inventory	10,800.00	
Prepaid Insurance	1,458.33	
Land	10,000.00	
Building	25,000.00	
Accumulated Depreciation—Building	(33.33)	
Truck	8,000.00	
Accumulated Depreciation—Truck	(133.33)	
Accounts Payable		$3,000.00
Interest Payable		133.33
Mortgage Payable (Long-Term)		20,000.00
Owner's Investment		60,000.00
Retained Earnings		2,808.34
	$85,941.67	$85,941.67

The closing process is a fairly routine one. It merely reverses the balances in the Income Statement accounts, bringing the ending balances to zero. Thus, since sales has a credit balance at the end of the accounting period, to close this account you must debit it to bring its balance to zero. Just the opposite happens with Cost of Goods Sold and all of the other Expenses; that is, they normally have a debit balance and to close them, they are credited for the same amount. Once all these debits and credits from the closed accounts are totaled on the trial balance, the difference should be a credit that is applied to Retained Earnings. This credit balance represents Net Income. If for some reason the debits are greater than the credits from the closed accounts this amount will represent a Net Loss.

In this chapter you have learned how to record business transactions into the original book of entry—the General Journal. You have also learned how to post to the accounting ledgers and how to make adjusting entries. Finally, you have learned how to close the accounting records of a company. In chapter 7 you will learn how the accounting for corporations differs from that of an individual proprietorship.

GLOSSARY

Accounts Receivable Write-Offs: The process of identifying an account receivable that is never going to be paid and taking it off the books. These accounts are written off to an Expense account with the amount being estimated by management based on past experiences of collection rates. When the entry is made, two accounts are created, an Expense account called Bad Debts Expense and a contra-Asset account (contra to Accounts Receivable).

Adjusting Journal Entries: Journal entries made at the end of the accounting period (month, quarter, and/or year) to recognize transactions that have occurred prior to the statements' issue date, but which have not yet been recorded in the journal. Examples of these entries include: depreciation; salaries earned, but not yet paid; adjustments to prepaid items, like insurance and interest on the mortgage which has not yet been paid.

Chart of Accounts: A listing of account numbers for each of the accounts. These numbers are usually divided into five groups; 100s for Assets, 200s for Liabilities, 300s for Owner's Equity, 400s for Revenues, and 500s for Expenses. Every time any accounting entry is made, the accountant will use the same account number for that particular Asset, Liability, Owner's Equity, Revenue, or Expense.

Closing Journal Entries: The process required to bring all accounts to a zero balance. This process is done at the end of the period (month, quarter, or year) prior to the preparation of the financial statements. Only Revenues and Expenses (also called temporary accounts) are closed and the difference between Revenues and Expenses is recorded as Net Income or net loss.

Credit: The right side of the amount column in a journal or ledger. Credits are recorded when Assets and Expenses are reduced and when Liabilities, Owner's Equity, and Revenue accounts are increased.

Debit: The left side of the amount column in a journal or ledger. Debits are recorded when Assets and Expenses are increased and when Liabilities, Owner's Equity, and Revenue accounts are decreased.

Depreciation: The process of spreading the historical cost of a Long-Term Asset over its useful life. In order to determine this amount, management must make an assumption as to the life of all of the Long-Term Assets. The historical cost is then spread evenly over this life expectancy. When this method of depreciation is used (evenly spread over the life) it is called the straight-line method of depreciation.

General Journal: The book in which transactions are first recorded, often referred to as "the book of original entry." As soon as a business transaction takes place, it is recorded in the general journal. The accounts impacted by the transaction: the date, the debits, credits, and an explanation of the transaction are also recorded.

General Ledger: A book containing a page (or pages) for every account in the business. After a transaction is recorded in the general journal, the components are then transferred (or posted) to the individual accounts in the general ledger. Thus, at any one time, one can review the individual accounts in the general ledger to determine their current balances.

Journal Entries: As soon as a business transaction occurs, an entry is made in the general journal to recognize this transaction. A debit (or debits) and a credit (or credits) will be made to the accounts that are impacted by this transaction. The debits and credits for each transaction will always be equal.

Posting: The process of transferring the information in the general journal to the individual accounts in the general ledger. At any time, one can review the individual accounts in the general ledger to determine their balances.

Trial Balance: A list of all accounts in the general ledger that have a balance other than zero. This is prepared right before the financial statements to make sure that the accounts are in balance and that all journal entries have been prepared correctly and accurately. If the trial balance does not balance (that is, debits do not equal credits), it indicates that there has been an error made in either the recording of the transactions, in the general journal, or in the posting of those transactions to the general ledger. (This does not include a trial balance, which has been completed after the closing of accounts.)

Chapter **7**

The Corporation

Up to this point we have been studying the Solana Beach Bicycle Company, which is an individual proprietorship. In other words, the business has one owner—Samantha. She has invested some of her own money into the company as well as borrowing some additional money.

Now Sam is thinking of growing her business. She has heard that by using other people's money, she will have more working capital and have the ability to expand the business. She has decided to investigate the possibility of incorporating her business and selling stock in her business.

But what is a corporation, really?

The Corporation Defined

A corporation has been defined as "an artificial being" independent from its owners, legally a separate entity. Corporations can be set up as for-profit or not-for-profit. For-profit corporations depend on making money in order to continue into the future. Not-for-profit corporations do not depend upon this profit to continue. These types of business, rather than depending on their profit, depend on gifts and grants from the public and private sectors for their continuation. Examples of not-for-profit corporations include charities, governmental, educational, and recreational organizations.

QUICK Tip

The Other Side of Incorporation: Although incorporation has many benefits, it should also be noted that the proprietor loses partial or majority control to the other stockholders. Also, the amount of paperwork and oversight increases. Before making the decision to incorporate you should seek professional advice from your accountant, lawyer, and financial advisor regarding the pros and cons.

A corporation is given the right to operate (a charter) from the state in which it incorporates, but the fact that a business is incorporated in one state, does not mean that it cannot operate in the others. Due to differing tax laws and the incorporation fees, some states have become more advantageous to incorporate in than others.

Characteristics of a Corporation

There are several characteristics that differentiate a corporation from other forms of business. One of the characteristics of a corporation that distinguishes it from a partnership or a proprietorship is that it has have limited liability. This means that the creditors of a corporation can lay claim only to the Assets of the corporation. Creditors of partnerships or proprietorships, on the other hand, can turn to the personal Assets of each owner whenever the Assets of the unincorporated firm are not sufficient to meet the creditors' claims. Because of this corporate characteristic, the states have laws that restrict the stockholders' right to withdraw Assets from the corporation. Each state has a law that prevents a corporation from paying dividends (that is, owners withdrawing Assets) whenever the net Assets (Assets minus Liabilities) are at or below a certain level. This minimum net Asset figure is often called the legal capital of a corporation.

Figure 7.1: CHARACTERISTICS OF A CORPORATION

- Is chartered as a legal and separate entity by an individual state
- Protects the personal Assets of the owners (stockholders) against creditors' claims (limited liability)
- Can issue capital stock to raise money
- Can issue dividends to stockholders
- May not issue dividends that would reduce the legal capital below a designated level

There are a number of reasons why a company would consider incorporation. Some of these reasons might include: 1) gaining the use of additional cash without the owner putting in his/her own personal funds; 2) removing legal liability from the individual and protecting his/her personal Assets; 3) securing various tax advantages. Incorporation may even provide the company with more credibility in the eyes of the business community and the general public.

What Is Capital Stock?

When a corporation receives its charter from the state, it also receives the right to sell a particular number of shares of stock to the public. Each share represents part ownership in the company. This number of shares the charter allows the corporation to sell is called the authorized shares. The corporation can sell as many shares as it chooses up to this authorized amount but no more. When the stock is initially sold to the public, the corporation will receive the money. After the initial sale, when the stock is sold from one individual to another (on a stock market such as the New York Stock Exchange or the NASDAQ), this money does not affect the Assets of the corporation.

The shareholders are jointly the owners of a corporation and can legally receive a distribution of the Assets of the corporation in two ways. First, the corporation can be liquidated—that is, all the Liabilities are paid off and the remaining Assets distributed to the shareholders, which means that the corporation ceases to operate; or second, the corporation can pay dividends.

Types of Capital Stock

Usually, two types of capital stock can be authorized by the state—common stock and preferred stock.

Figure 7.2: SOME CHARACTERISTICS OF COMMON STOCK AND PREFERRED STOCK

- Common stockholders have the right to vote for the directors of the corporation; preferred shareholders usually do not.

- Preferred shareholders have first claim to dividends; that is, in any year when dividends are declared by the board of directors, preferred shareholders must be allocated their share of the dividends before the common stockholders are entitled to any.

- The preferred shareholders have a fixed claim to dividends during any one year, whereas, the common shareholders' claims are not fixed.

- In the event the corporation is liquidated (that is, its Assets sold, Liabilities paid off, and the remaining cash distributed to the shareholders), the preferred shareholders' claim to the corporate Assets takes precedence over those of the common shareholders.

- Most preferred stock is cumulative. This means that if the preferred shareholders are not paid their full dividend in any year, in subsequent years dividend payments to the preferred shareholders must be sufficient to cover the previously inadequate dividend payments before any dividends can be paid to the common stockholders.

The common and preferred stock may or may not have a par value; par value is the value assigned to each share by a corporation in its corporate charter. If a stock has a par value, that value appears on the stock certificate (for example, $1 par or $5 par or $100 par, and so on). Stock rarely, if ever, is initially sold by a corporation for less than par value, either because state laws prevent such a sale or because the laws allow the creditors of the corporation to hold stockholders personally liable to the extent of any such discount.

In many states the total par value of all stock sold will be the corporation's legal capital. In some states, however, a corporation's legal capital is equal to the total amount received when the stock is initially sold. This can vary since par value stock is often sold for more than the par value figure. This legal capital amount is an important figure because a corporation may not issue dividends that would cause the net Assets (Assets-Liabilities) to go below the amount of this legal capital.

Understanding Dividend Calculations: A 10 percent Common Stock with a par value of $100, should receive a $10 dividend each year. A 10 percent Preferred Stock with a par value of $100, should also receive a $10 dividend each year. But if only $6 is paid in dividends in year one, then the next year, the remaining $4 plus the $10 for year two must be paid to cumulative preferred stockholders before the common stockholders receive any further dividend.

When dividends on cumulative preferred stock are not paid, those dividends are said to be in arrears, and a footnote must be added to the financial statements indicating the amount of the dividends in arrears. The Balance Sheet will not show dividends in arrears as a Liability. Some preferred stock is non-cumulative, which means that if a year passes and the preferred stockholders do not receive a dividend, those shareholders never receive that dividend payment.

Some preferred stock is participating preferred, which mean that the preferred shareholders' claim to dividends in any one year is not rigidly fixed. Those shareholders, in certain "good" years, will share with the common shareholders in the "excess" dividend payments. The amount or percentage of dividends that the preferred shareholders can receive in excess of the amount to which they have a prior claim varies considerably from company to company and is determined by the board of directors.

QUIZ

Assume that the Blanca Corporation has 10,000 shares of cumulative, participating, preferred stock outstanding. There are 20,000 shares of 10 percent Common Stock, and they will each receive $10 per share in dividends. This preferred stock is also 10 percent, with a $100 par value. The Preferred Stock participates at the 30 percent level, meaning that these stockholders will receive 30 percent of whatever excess dividends are left over after the initial dividends have been paid. The dividend declared by the board of directors this year is $500,000. How much in total do the preferred and common stockholders receive in dividends this year?

See page 121 for answers.

The Stockholders' Equity Section of the Balance Sheet

As you recall from chapter 3, the Owner's Equity Section of the Balance Sheet contains two items, Owner's Investment and Retained Earnings. The only difference on the books of a corporation is that the Owner's Investment is replaced with Common Stock and Preferred Stock and this section is called the Stockholders' Equity section in a privately-owned company. The reason for this is that the stockholders are the owners of the corporation.

Dividends and Splits

In general, a corporation cannot pay a dividend when such action would reduce the corporation's capital below its legal capital figure. Usually, dividends can be paid, but only to the extent of the total Retained Earnings, i.e., the profit that has been retained in the business.

In addition, a corporation obviously cannot pay a cash dividend unless it has the cash to do so, and the cash is not needed for other purposes. Often, a corporation has sizable Retained Earnings as a result of successful operations in the past, but very little cash, which reduces its ability to pay dividends.

There are two goals of a corporation, 1) to maximize Net Income and 2) to satisfy the stockholders with the increase in their stock price or with the future expectation of a stock price increase. The act of issuing a cash dividend is like a double-edged sword. On the one hand, it will satisfy the immediate needs of the stockholders to receive cash, but on the other hand it will deplete cash in the company for future investment and growth. Therefore, management needs to carefully adjust this balance to satisfy both the short- and long-term goals of the stockholders.

Dividends without Cash

Stock Dividends

Dividends can be divided into two categories, cash and stock. Companies often declare and issue stock dividends instead of cash dividends. Only when the board of directors declares dividends do they become legal liabilities of the corporation. Once the dividends are declared, the corporation is legally required to pay these dividends or issue the additional shares within a specified period of time. When stock dividends are issued, the corporation will issue additional shares of stock in the corporation to each shareholder instead of cash.

There are several reasons why a corporation may issue stock dividends instead of cash. There may not be sufficient cash to pay a cash dividend, so rather than not issuing any dividends that year at all, the board may decide to issue the stock dividend instead. Another reason for issuing the stock dividend might be that the company needs the cash for other purposes. If, for instance, they are planning an expansion of operations to Brazil and need to accumulate cash in order to begin the new operation, they can issue stock dividends in order to keep sufficient levels of cash necessary for the expansion.

Alert!

Restrictions on Issuing Stock Dividends: In order for a corporation to issue stock dividends it must have enough authorized stock that has not been issued. If it does not, the corporation will have to apply for the issuing of more stock from the Secretary of State in the state in which the corporation is incorporated.

Stock Splits

A company can also declare a stock split instead of issuing cash dividends. The stock split increases the number of shares outstanding and decreases the stocks' par value. Stock may be split in a variety of ways—for example, two for one; three for one; three for two; and so on. (In a two for one stock split, each share becomes two shares. In a three for two stock split, every two shares becomes three shares. So, for example, a stockholder who held ten shares would have fifteen shares after the split.) Whether the company issues a stock dividend or a stock split, it must have the additional shares authorized by the state prior to the issue. If the company already has an amount of authorized shares that have not yet been issued, then this is unnecessary. If a company had ten thousand shares authorized when they were chartered, and have only issued three thousand shares to date but not enough stock remains from the initial authorization, the company must request a larger authorization from the state.

A company may split its stock for several reasons. One reason is that a stock split increases the number of shares on the market, which may mean that, in time, more people will own a part of the company. It is desirable to have more investors because it creates more interest in the company's stock, as well as in the company, which has the potential of driving up the stock price and getting more capital invested into the company as well. Another reason for a stock split is that increasing the number of shares reduces the price per share; thus, again, more people are able to buy the shares. Yet another reason is that many people would rather buy one hundred shares of $50 stock than fifty shares of $100 stock even though the amount they would spend and the proportion of the company they would own would be the same. One reason for this decision is that the brokerage fee on round lots (one hundred shares or multiples thereof) is less than on odd lots (less than one hundred shares).

Incorporating Solana Beach Bicycle Company

Sale of Stock

Well, now, Samantha has heard all of these definitions, and the prospect of getting more capital into her business is very interesting to her. By incorporating, she is able to expand her business without putting any more of her own money into it. She incorporates her business using close to the same name as before, so as not to confuse her current customers, and calls the business—The Solana Beach Bicycle Corporation.

When the new corporation sells stock, cash is increased (if the stock was sold for cash), and the common stock account is increased by the same amount. For example, when 120,000 shares of Common Stock with Par Value of $50 is sold for $60 per share cash, cash is increased $7,200,000, the common stock account increases $6,000,000 (120,000 shares x $50 par value), and another account called Paid-in Capital-Common (or Capital in Excess of Par) is increased by $1,200,000. This Capital in Excess of Par amount represents any amount paid into the corporation over and above the par value of the stock. This account is also part of Stockholders' Equity.

You may be wondering why the amount paid for the stock in the example above is higher than the par value. Remember that the par value was simply a value assigned to each share of stock when the business was incorporated. By law in most states, the stock cannot be sold for below par, but can be sold for more than par value. The stock, when it is finally issued on the market, will almost always sell at above par, causing the account Paid-in Capital in Excess of Par to be created.

The impact on the Balance Sheet is shown in Figure 7.3:

Figure 7.3

Current Assets:	**Stockholders' Equity:**
Cash . . . .+$7,200,000	Common Stock, $50 Par . . . .+$6,000,000
	Paid-in Capital in Excess of Par, Common . .+$1,200,000
	$7,200,000

When stock does not have a par value, but the Board of Directors has assigned a stated value to the no-par stock, the stock sale transaction is accounted for in a manner similar to that shown in the Figure 7.3. The amount added to the common stock account equals the total stated value of the stock sold and any excess is added to the paid-in-capital account, now called Paid-in Capital in Excess of Stated Value, Common. The sale of preferred stock would cause the same changes as shown in the example, with the exception that the title of the accounts would be Preferred Stock and Paid-in Capital in Excess of Par, Preferred instead.

When stock has neither a par value nor a stated value, the common stock account is increased by whatever amount is realized upon the sale of the stock. For example, if ten shares of no-par common stock sells for $100, the common stock and cash accounts are both increased by $100; if ten more shares are sold for $115 a few days later, the common stock account increases another $115, and so on.

Payment of Cash Dividends

When the board of directors declares cash dividends, the Retained Earnings figure is decreased and dividends payable, a Current Liability, is increased. For example if a corporation has 150,000 shares of common stock outstanding and the board of directors declares a $.20 dividend, the Retained Earnings would decrease by $30,000 and the dividends payable would increase by $30,000 (150,000 shares x $.20). The Balance Sheet changes are shown in Figure 7.4. The Income Statement is not affected at all by this declaration.

Figure 7.4: **BALANCE SHEET CHANGES**

Current Liabilities:

Dividends Payable . . . .+$30,000

Stockholders' Equity:

Common Stock XXX

Retained Earnings . . . .−$30,000

Total Liabilities and Stockholders' Equity . . . . No Change

When the dividend is actually paid, cash is decreased and dividends payable is decreased. Continuing the preceding example, when the dividend is paid, cash would decrease $30,000 and the Liability called "dividends payable" would be eliminated from the Balance Sheet.

Financial statements are affected in the same manner when cash dividends are declared and paid to preferred shareholders.

Stock Dividends Declared and Issued

Assume the Solana Beach Bicycle Corporation's Stockholders' Equity section looked like the one in Figure 7.5 after the corporation has been in operation for a while:

Figure 7.5

Stockholders' Equity:

Common Stock, $50 Par $10,000,000

Paid-in Capital in Excess of Par, Common 3,500,000

$13,500,000

Retained Earnings 10,000,000

Total Stockholders' Equity $23,500,000

The corporation declared and issued a 10 percent stock dividend when its stock was selling on the market for $200 per share. We can tell from the Stockholders' Equity section that the corporation had two hundred thousand shares of common stock outstanding prior to the stock dividend ($10,000,000 common stock/$50 par = 200,000 shares). A 10 percent stock dividend will increase the number of shares by 20,000 (10 percent of 200,000 = 20,000). Since the market price of each share is $200, the Retained Earnings account is decreased by $4,000,000 (20,000 shares x $200 = $4,000,000), the common stock account is increased by $1,000,000, (20,000 shares x $50 Par = $1,000,000), and the paid-in capital account is increased by the difference which is $3,000,000. The journal entry would look like this:

Dr.: Retained Earnings $4,000,000
Cr.: Common Stock $1,000,000 .
Cr.: Paid-in Capital in Excess of Par, Common $3,000,000

Alert!

Stock Dividends and Retained Earnings: Issuing stock dividends affects the corporation's Retained Earnings in exactly the same way as if it were a cash dividend. The only difference is that additional stock is being distributed to the stockholders instead of cash. Since it has the same impact on Retained Earnings, however, the corporation must still have sufficient Retained Earnings to make this declaration.

The equity section of the Balance Sheet appears as shown in Figure 7.6 after the stock dividend:

Figure 7.6

Stockholders' Equity:

Common Stock, $50 Par $11,000,000

Paid-in Capital in Excess of Par, Common 6,500,000

$17,500,000

Retained Earnings 6,000,000

Total Stockholders' Equity $23,500,000

Notice that the total Stockholders' Equity ($23,500,000) does not change. Furthermore, neither the Assets nor the Liabilities of the corporation are affected by a stock dividend nor are the income or Expense items.

The accounting for a stock dividend is somewhat different whenever the dividend is greater than 20 percent to 25 percent of the shares previously outstanding.

Whenever such large stock dividends are issued, the market value of the stock is not relevant in determining the change in the Balance Sheet figures. Instead, the Retained Earnings are reduced by the par value of the new shares.

Had Solana Beach Bicycle Corporation in the example shown in Figure 7.6 declared and issued a 50 percent instead of a 10 percent stock dividend, for example, the Balance Sheet would have been changed to look like the example in Figure 7.7. Since there are 200,000 shares outstanding in Figure 7.5, a 50 percent stock dividend would entail the issuing of an additional 100,000 shares. (There would be no change to the Paid-in Capital in Excess of Par, Common amount from Figure 7.5.)

Figure 7.7

Stockholders' Equity:

Common Stock, $50 Par	$15,000,000
Paid-in Capital in Excess of Par, Common	3,500,000
	$18,500,000
Retained Earnings	5,000,000
Total Stockholders' Equity	$23,500,000

Notice that Total Stockholders' Equity does not change from Figure 7.5 because all we have done is shift dollars out of Retained Earnings into Common Stock.

Now assume that the board of directors of the Solana Beach Bicycle Corporation above declared a two-for-one stock split instead of a 50 percent stock dividend. Four hundred thousand shares (remember, there were two hundred thousand shares outstanding) of new $25 par stock would have been sent to the shareholders and the old $50 par stock would have been called in so that only the $25 stocks are held by shareholders. The Stockholders' Equity section of the Balance Sheet would now look like Figure 7.8:

Figure 7.8

Stockholders' Equity:

Common Stock, $25 Par	$10,000,000
Paid-in Capital in Excess of Par, Common	3,500,000
	$13,500,000
Retained Earnings	10,000,000
Total Stockholders' Equity	$23,500,000

Notice that there are no differences in this partial Balance Sheet and the one shown in Figure 7.5 (before the stock split) except that the par value has changed from $50 to $25 and the number of shares outstanding has changed from 200,000 to 400,000.

What Is Treasury Stock?

When a corporation buys back its own stock and does not cancel it or resell it, it is known as treasury stock. A corporation may buy its own stock for a variety of reasons. For example, it may need the stock to distribute for stock dividends or to satisfy a stock option contract with its employees.

Purchase of Treasury Stock

To begin, operation Solana Beach Bicycle Corporation sold one hundred thousand shares of $50 par stock for $60 each on July 1, 2007, the day Solana Beach Bicycle began doing business as a corporation. Two years later, it buys back ten thousand shares of its own stock for $700,000 (notice that the price of the stock has increased from the original sale price of $60 to $70). Until this stock is legally canceled or resold, it is known as treasury stock.

Before the Solana Beach Bicycle Corporation acquired its own stock, its Stockholders' Equity section of the Balance Sheet looked like Figure 7.9:

Figure 7.9	
Stockholders' Equity:	
Common Stock, $50 Par (120,000 shares)	.$6,000,000
Paid-in Capital in Excess of Par, Common	.1,200,000
	$7,200,000
Retained Earnings	.10,000,000
Total Stockholders' Equity	.$17,200,000

After the Solana Beach Bicycle Corporation acquired ten thousand shares of its own stock, its Stockholders' Equity section of the Balance Sheet looked like Figure 7.10:

Figure 7.10

Stockholders' Equity:

Common Stock, $50 Par

(10,000 Shares of which are Treasury Stock) $6,000,000

Paid-in Capital, Common 1,200,000

$7,200,000

Retained Earnings (See Footnote 1) 10,000,000

$17,200,000

Less: Cost of Treasury Stock . . . .(700,000)

Total Stockholders' Equity $16,500,000

The following footnote would be included below the Balance Sheet of the current year:

Footnote 1: Although the Retained Earnings totals $10,000,000, the acquisition of treasury stock has reduced the Retained Earnings available for dividends by $700,000, the cost of the treasury stock; thus, the Solana Beach Bicycle Corporation may legally declare and pay dividends of not more than $9,300,000 ($10,000,000 Retained Earnings – $700,000 Treasury Stock).

You should be aware of several changes caused by the purchase of the treasury stock:

- The total Stockholders' Equity has decreased from $17,200,000 to $16,500,000. The Balance Sheet is still in balance because cash has decreased by the same amount $700,000 (the amount of cash paid for the purchase of the treasury stock).

- A treasury stock purchase reduces the Retained Earnings of a company and as a result reduces the amount of dividends the corporation can pay. A corporation usually cannot buy treasury stock unless its Retained Earnings is equal to or exceeds the cost of the treasury stock. This restriction is necessary to prevent a corporation from reducing its capital below its required legal capital figure.

- The Balance Sheet would not be complete without some notation in the Stockholders' Equity section of the statement regarding the reduction of Retained Earnings due to treasury stock, as is accomplished by the footnote in Figure 7.10 above.

- The number of shares of common stock now outstanding is 110,000 shares (the number of shares *issued* has not changed from the original 120,000).

Alert!

Treasury Stock Is NOT an Asset: The purchase of the stock by the corporation merely reduces the amount that the owners have invested in the business.

If cash dividends were declared today, they would be paid only to the owners of the 110,000 shares; the company would not pay dividends to itself on the ten thousand shares of treasury stock. Dividends are paid only on outstanding stock, and treasury stock is not considered to be outstanding. Each corporation is authorized to issue a maximum number of shares as specified in the corporate charter. The number of shares authorized can be greater than or equal to the number of shares issued, but a corporation can issue no more shares than authorized. Most firms show the number of shares authorized, issued, and outstanding, in the Stockholders' Equity section of the Balance Sheet. For example, before the purchase of the treasury stock the Solana Beach Bicycle Corporation's Stockholders' Equity section would look like Figure 7.11:

Figure 7.11

Stockholders' Equity:

Common Stock, $50 Par

Authorized 500,000 Shares

Issued & Outstanding 120,000 Shares $6,000,000

Paid-in Capital in Excess of Par, Common 1,200,000

$7,200,000

Retained Earnings 10,000,000

Total Stockholders' Equity $17,200,000

After the purchase of the ten thousand shares of treasury stock, the Solana Beach Bicycle Corporation's Stockholders' Equity section would look like Figure 7.12:

Figure 7.12

Stockholders' Equity:

Common Stock, $50 Par (10,000 shares of which are Treasury Stock)

Authorized 500,000 Shares

Issued 120,000 Shares

Outstanding 110,000 Shares $6,000,000

Paid-in Capital in Excess of Par, Common 1,200,000

$7,200,000

Retained Earnings (See Footnote 1) 10,000,000

$17,200,000

Less: Cost of Treasury Stock . . . .(700,000)

Total Stockholders' Equity $16,500,000

Footnote 1: Although the Retained Earnings total $10,000,000, the Solana Beach Bicycle Corporation may legally declare and pay dividends of not more than $9,300,000. The acquisition of treasury stock has reduced the Retained Earnings available for dividends by $700,000, the cost of the treasury stock.

Notice above that the number of shares issued and authorized has not changed since the purchase of the treasury stock. The only change is to the number of shares outstanding. Even though the treasury stock is no longer outstanding, those shares are considered to still be part of the issued shares of the corporation.

Selling the Treasury Stock

The company can either hold, sell, or cancel its treasury stock. If the Solana Beach Bicycle Corporation sold four thousand shares of its treasury stock for $80 per share the journal entry to record this sales transaction would be:

Debit: Cash $320,000
Credit: Treasury Stock $280,000
       (4,000 shares x the original cost of $70 per share)
Credit: Paid-in Capital in Excess of Cost, Treasury $40,000

After the sale of the four thousand shares of treasury stock the Stockholders' Equity section would look like Figure 7.13:

Figure 7.13

Stockholders' Equity:

Common Stock, $50 Par (6,000 shares of which are Treasury Stock)

Authorized 500,000 Shares

Issued 120,000 Shares

Outstanding 114,000 Shares $6,000,000

Paid-in Capital in Excess of Par, Common 1,200,000

Paid-in Capital in Excess of Cost, Treasury 40,000

$7,240,000

Retained Earnings (See Footnote 1) 10,000,000

$17,240,000

Less: Cost of Treasury Stock ....(420,000)

Total Stockholders' Equity $16,820,000

You should be aware of several changes caused by the sale of the treasury stock:

- The total Stockholders' Equity increased (from Figure 7.12) by $320,000—the amount of cash received for the sale of the treasury stock.
- The Treasury Stock account decreased by only $280,000, the amount the four thousand shares had cost the company when they were purchased: 4,000 shares x $70 per share. (Remember, the company bought these shares at the market rate of $70 per share.)
- The sale of Treasury Stock for more than it cost (bought at $70 per share and sold for $80 per share, so the original cost to the corporation was $280,000 while the sales price was $320,000) did not result in a profit of $40,000. The rules of accounting do not allow a corporation to make a profit on the sale of its own stock. The Income Statement is not affected by the transaction; the Retained Earnings do not change; and the $40,000 simply creates a new Balance Sheet account that is called Paid-In Capital in excess of Cost, Treasury. This account is somewhat like the

Paid-in Capital, Common account that results when stock is initially sold for more than its par value.

Selling Treasury Stock: When treasury stock is sold for less than it cost, the Paid-In Capital, Treasury account is reduced. If this account does not exist or if the account is not large enough to absorb the difference between the sales prices and the cost of the treasury stock, the Paid-In Capital in Excess of Par, Common is reduced. If this account is not sufficient then Retained Earnings is reduced.

In this chapter, you have learned about how the financial statements in a corporation differ from those of a proprietorship. You have also learned about the corporate structure and how individual transactions affect the financial statements of a corporation. In chapter 8 you will be introduced to how to use financial statements for short-term decision making.

ANSWER

Preferred Stock

10,000 Shares x $10 = $100,000

Common Stock

20,000 Shares x $10 = $200,000

Remainder to be divided =

$500,000 – $100,000 – $200,000 = $200,000

30 percent of Remainder = $60,000

70 percent of Remainder = $140,000

Total for P.S. = $160,000

Total for C.S. = $340,000

GLOSSARY

Arrears: The amount of money that has not been paid on cumulative preferred stock. Since the stock is cumulative, in most cases, the dividends for common stock and other non-cumulative preferred stock may not be paid until the dividends in arrears have been paid.

Authorized Shares: The number of shares a state allows a corporation to issue to the public when the company is incorporated. If a corporation needs or wants to issue more stock than authorized in order to raise more capital, it must request the authorization of additional shares.

Capital Stock: A term used to refer to both the Common and Preferred Stock of a corporation, which the company is initially authorized to issue when it receives its incorporation charter.

Cash Dividends: Dividends declared by the board of directors and paid in cash to stockholders. These become a Liability on the corporation's Balance Sheet when they are declared by the Board of Directors. The corporation must have sufficient Retained Earnings and cash to make this declaration. After the declaration, once dividends are paid, cash and Retained Earnings are reduced.

Common Stock: One of the two types of stock that a corporation can issue to the public when it is chartered by the state. Common stock usually does not have a defined dividend amount per year, but only receives dividends when they are declared by the board of directors. Common stockholders usually have voting rights to elect the board of directors.

Corporation: An incorporated business is "an artificial being" independent from its owners. It is a legal separate entity. A company will request permission to exist from the secretary of state of any state. Once it has been granted the charter to operate, it may sell stock in order to raise capital.

Cumulative Preferred Stock: When holders of this type of stock are not paid a full dividend in any year (usually this dividend amount will be stated on the share of stock), then subsequent years' dividend payments to them must be sufficient to cover the current year as well as the amount that was not paid in any previous years, before any dividends can be paid to the common stockholders. (See also Preferred Stock.)

Legal Capital: In many states, this is the total par value of all stock sold. In some states, however, a corporation's legal capital is equal to the total amount of money received when the stock is initially sold. Thus, in this second case, the legal capital would be equal to the par value and the paid in capital in excess of par.

Paid-in Capital in Excess of Par: The amount of money received by a corporation from the sale of stock above the par value. In some states, it is both the par value and the paid in capital in excess of par that represents the legal capital of the corporation.

Par Value: The value assigned by a corporation to each share of stock, common or preferred, when it is incorporated. In most states, the common stock cannot be sold at below par. Generally, stock sells for more than the par value rather than at the par value itself.

Participating Preferred Stock: Preferred stockholders, in certain "good" years, will share with the common shareholders in the "excess" dividend payments. For example, after the preferred stockholders receive their 10 percent dividend, and the common stockholders receive their declared amount of dividend, if there is money left in total declaration for the year, the common and the preferred will share in that amount. If preferred stock is not participating, the total remaining amount will go to the common stockholders. (See also Preferred Stock.)

Preferred Stock: One of the two types of stock that a corporation can issue upon receiving its charter from the state. This type of stock has preference over the Common Stockholders for when dividends are issued and also will receive its money back from the corporation first if there is a liquidation. (See also Cumulative Preferred Stock and Participating Preferred Stock.)

Stock Dividends: Dividends declared by the board of directors and issued to the stockholders in the form of additional shares of stock rather than cash. The corporation must have sufficient Retained Earnings and authorized stock to make this declaration.

Stock Split: A stock split is declared by the board of directors to split the number of shares that a stockholder currently holds. These splits can be for two for one, three for one, etc. The corporation must have a sufficient number of authorized shares to make the split. Often, stock splits are declared by the board of directors when the price of the stock is very high and the corporation wants to encourage more stockholders in the corporation by lowering the price of each share.

Treasury Stock: The corporation's own stock that it holds when it buys shares back from existing stockholders. This stock remains on the books of the issuing corporation until it cancels the stock or resells the shares back to the public. Treasury stock appears on the Balance Sheet as a reduction of Retained Earnings.

Chapter 8

Using Financial Statements for Short-Term Analysis

▶ **Using Short-Term Ratios**

▶ **Current and Quick Ratios**

▶ **Working Capital**

▶ **Composition of Assets**

Using Short-Term Ratios

Financial statements can be extremely useful for evaluating a company's future in the near-term (usually defined as one to twelve months) as well as beyond the near-term. This chapter will focus on near-term evaluation; evaluation beyond the near-term will be the focus of chapter 9.

The most important question to be answered when evaluating a company's near-term future is whether or not the company will be able to pay its debts when they come due. If the firm cannot, it may be forced into bankruptcy or perhaps even forced to cease operations. As you learned earlier, even a profitable company can become short on cash and place its future in jeopardy.

Certain financial statement users will be particularly interested in the short-term prospects of a company. Bankers, for example, who have made or are contemplating making short-term loans (thirty-day, sixty-day, or even six-month loans) are mainly concerned with determining whether the borrowing company will be able to repay their loans when they come due. These statement users will attempt to forecast the company's cash flow for the period of time during which their loans are expected to be outstanding. For this reason, the cash flow statement discussed in chapter 5 becomes very important.

Even those users who are mostly interested in the short-term, will also have an interest in the long-term. Again taking banks as an example, bankers must be aware of what is happening now and what the future looks like for all of their customers in order to decide to whom they can loan money and in order to estimate their own future cash flows.

Figure 8.1 gives some examples of how certain financial statement users might use short-term ratios.

Figure 8.1: HOW SHORT-TERM RATIOS ARE USED

Users	Ratios	Used For
Bankers	Current Ratio	To make short-term loans
	Working Capital	
Vendors	Quick Ratio	To extend credit for purchases
	Inventory Turnover	

Users	Ratios	Used For
Credit Card Company	Current Ratio	To issue credit cards
	Working Capital	
Business Owners	All	On-going short-term analysis of their businesses

There are a number of key figures that are useful in these assessments. They are highlighted in Figure 8.1 and listed below in Figure 8.2.

Figure 8.2: KEY SHORT-TERM RATIOS

Ratio	Calculation
Current Ratio	Current Assets/Current Liabilities
Quick Ratio	Quick Asset/Current Liabilities
	[Quick Assets = Current Assets − Inventory − Prepaid Items]
Working Capital	Current Assets − Current Liabilities
Inventory Turnover Ratio	Cost of Goods Sold/Average Inventory
	[Average Inventory = (Beginning Inventory + Ending Inventory)/2]
Average Collection Period	Accounts Receivable/Average Sales per day
	(Average Sales/Day = Annual Sales/365)

Current and Quick Ratios

To figure out whether a company is going to survive in the short-term, you should look first at the Balance Sheet. Compare the company's Current Assets with their Current Liabilities (debts that must be paid within twelve months) using the current ratio.

Current Ratio = Current or Short-Term Assets/Current or Short-Term Liabilities

Also widely used is the comparison of the firm's quick Assets—those Current Assets that can be quickly turned into cash—to the Current Liabilities. Usually quick Assets include cash, current receivables, and marketable securities, or in other words, Currents Assets minus Inventory and prepaid items. This ratio of quick Assets to Current Liabilities is referred to as the quick (or acid test) ratio.

Quick Asset Ratio = Quick Assets/Current or Short-Term Liabilities

Referring to Figure 3.4 in chapter 3, the current ratio for the Solana Beach Bicycle Company would be 12.6. This is calculated by dividing the Short-Term Assets on December 31, 2006, of $50,385 by the Short-Term Liabilities on the same day of $4,000. Again using the values from Figure 3.4, the quick ratio for the bicycle company would be 6.6. This is calculated by taking the quick Assets on December 31, 2006, of $26,385 and dividing them by the Current Liabilities of $4,000. But what do these numbers mean?

Before you can decide whether a firm has sufficient Current Assets or quick Assets to cover their Current Liabilities, you need to know what the current and quick ratios were in the preceding periods. The rule of thumb is that the current ratio should be greater than 2.0. What this means is that the Current Assets available to the company to pay their debts are at least double their Current Liabilities. The quick Asset ratio rule of thumb is that this ratio should be 1.5 or larger. These ratios vary from industry to industry, and therefore your company's current ratio should not only be compared to prior years and to the rule of thumb figure, but should also be compared to similar companies in the same industry.

In general, the larger the current and quick ratios are the greater the probability that a company will be able to pay its debts in the near term. In the case of the Solana Beach Bicycle Company, the current and quick ratios are well above the rule of thumb, which means the business is in a very good position to be able to pay its Current Liabilities.

Bigger Isn't Always Better: These ratios can also be too large. A company's profitability is reduced whenever it has too large a proportion of any particular type of Asset including cash. A current or quick ratio that is way over the industry average may be an indication that this is the case.

Knowing the environmental conditions that existed in prior periods as compared to now and having data about similar companies in the same industry are also useful. You can get the average ratios for various industries from publications such as *Moody's, Standard & Poor, Dun & Bradstreet*, or *Robert Morris Associates*.

QUICK Tip

Stay Informed: Unfortunately, there is no easy or shortcut method for obtaining the information on present and past environmental conditions. You must read widely and be sensitive to changes in the marketplace.

Working Capital

Another important factor to consider in the short-term in addition to these two ratios is the firms' working capital. This is calculated by subtracting the Current Liabilities from the Current Assets.

$$\text{Working Capital} = \text{Current or Short-Term Assets} - \text{Current or Short-Term Liabilities}$$

Working capital is a cushion. It allows management to make errors in its estimate of future cash receipts and disbursements and still be able to pay its debts when they fall due. For example, if management estimates both cash receipts and disbursements for the next thirty days to be $30,000, and for some reason receipts only total $25,000 and disbursements total $35,000, the firm must have either sufficient working capital at the beginning of the month to cover the shortfall or good credit with its bankers. If this is not the case it will find itself unable to settle its debts and possibly be out of business or with the creditors taking control.

It's All Relative: How do we know what is a good enough cushion? The calculation of working capital will not help a great deal unless it is related to the firm's cash flow and to prior year's figures. For example, calculating a working capital of $20,000 does not mean anything by itself. However, to know that working capital three years ago was $10,000, two years ago was $14,000, and last year was $17,000 indicates a positive trend that gives more meaning to this year's figure of $20,000. Also important is the economy, the budget for future Current Liabilities, and the need to have excess cash in the business.

In addition, it is necessary to compare the working capital to the cash flow of the firm, as you calculated in chapter 5. How much working capital a firm should have depends upon its cash flow. It makes sense that a business that receives and/or disburses an average of $7,000,000 per week, should have a larger working capital balance than a firm that receives and/or disburses $7,000 per week because the first business' needs for cash are higher.

In the case of our bicycle company, the working capital cushion is very good. It is $46,385 (Current Assets of $50,385 minus the Current Liabilities of $4,000).

QUICK Tip

Working Capital Cushion: Is your working capital cushion large enough? What is your cash flow per month? Is it ever negative? What is your cash flow budget for the future? If you had a normal negative flow of cash in the past, and you have projected a negative flow of cash for the next twelve months, you will need a larger working capital cushion than if your projections are the opposite. Also, what are your predictions for the economy over the next twelve months? If you expect a slow down that might affect your industry and company, you will want to have a larger cushion for working capital since you will likely have less Revenue coming in to help you cover your debts.

Composition of Assets

In deciding whether a company is going to survive the near-term, you also want to look at the composition of their Current Assets; that is, you want to see that each of the various Current Asset items is a desirable size. Your main interest here centers on receivables and Inventory items.

Inventories and receivables sometimes may become too large. Receivables may become too large because customers delay their payments or because the company changed its credit policy so that sales are made to people or firms who are greater credit risks or who are slower in paying off their debts. Inventories get too large when, for example, management overestimates the demand for the company's products and either buys or makes too many items. These situations have negative implications for the near-term business prospects. To determine whether inventories are a reasonable size, you can calculate the Inventory turnover ratio.

Inventory Turnover Ratio

Inventory turnover ratio is calculated by dividing Cost of Goods Sold by the average Inventory.

Inventory Turnover Ratio = Cost of Goods Sold/Average Inventory

Average Inventory is defined as (beginning Inventory balance + ending Inventory balance)/2. This represents the number of times that the Inventory "turned over" (was sold during a particular period of time). If a business sells and replaces its stock of Inventory at a rapid rate, turnover is high; if items sit without being sold for long periods, Inventory turnover is low. There is no widely used rule of thumb available. To decide whether the Inventory turnover figure for a firm is desirable, you must look at previous turnover figures of the firm, turnover figures of other similar firms, and industry wide averages. A relatively high turnover figure would suggest that sales are being lost due to shortage of Inventory; a low turnover figure may suggest that demand for the goods is falling, that some of the Inventory cannot be sold, or that prices must be reduced. A low turnover figure may also indicate that as of the Balance Sheet date too much cash has been invested in Inventory items.

In a grocery store, you would expect to see an Inventory turnover of one to two days because the Inventory is perishable. In a fur coat boutique, on the other hand, you would expect this ratio to be one or two months since fur coats are bought much less frequently and in much smaller quantities than foodstuffs. It is critical to know and understand the industry you are analyzing in order to be able to evaluate the ratios.

What would you want the Inventory turnover ratio be for the Solana Beach Bicycle Company? Their Inventory certainly will not move as fast as the perishable commodities in a grocery store; however, if they are going to stay in business and not end up with a lot of Inventory that they can't sell, it should move faster than the fur coats discussed above. So what do you think? One week? One month? Two Months? Let's see.

To find the Cost of Goods Sold, we need to move to Figure 4.1 in chapter 4. On December 31, 2006, the Cost of Goods Sold was $14,200.

Then to calculate the average Inventory, we go back to Figure 3.4 in chapter 3, and see that Inventory on December 31, 2006, is $23,000. What was Inventory on December 31, 2005? Well, the bicycle company was not in business then, so it was zero. Now to calculate the average Inventory of beginning ($0) and ending ($23,000), we add these two numbers together and divide by two. Thus, average Inventory is $11,500.

To arrive at Inventory turnover, we divide Cost of Goods Sold ($14,200) by average Inventory ($11,500) and arrive at 1.24. What does this mean?

Well, it means that Inventory is turning over on the average of 1.24 times per year. That is about every twelve months. Not good! The bicycles are being built and/or bought, and then not sold for twelve months. If this ratio is not improved, the company is going to have a lot of money tied up in Inventory, since it's not getting it back for a long time—nearly one year. She may need a better marketing plan. Or it may be that there is just too much Inventory in the shop for what can be sold at this location. What other possibilities do you see?

Average Collection Period

To determine whether the balance in Accounts Receivable is too large (or too small), you can calculate the average collection period.

Average collection period = Accounts receivable/average sales per day

(Average sales per day is equal to Annual Sales/365 days.)

You must rely more on the firm's previous average collection period figures in evaluating the result and less on the figures of other firms and industry-wide figures in this case because firms' credit policies and their mix of cash sales and sales on account differ widely. If the average collection period has been increasing, it may indicate the firm's increasing difficulty in collecting its receivables as they come due.

Once again, let's look at the Solana Beach Bicycle Company and see how they are doing in collecting their receivables. To find Accounts Receivable we go to Figure 3.4 and see that at the end of 2006, Accounts Receivable is $9,000 (This is net receivables: Accounts Receivable minus allowance for doubtful accounts.) Then we look at Figure 4.1 and see that sales for the year 2006 are $35,500. To arrive at average sales per day, we divide $35,500 by 365 days and get $97.26. To arrive at the average collection period we divide the Accounts Receivable $9,000 by the average sales per day of $97.26 and get a number of 92.5. This means that it is taking the company ninety-two and one-half days to collect their receivables. Solana Beach Bicycle Company has a policy that generally gives customers thirty to sixty days to pay. The fact that the average collection period for Solana Beach

Bicycle is longer than this means that it is taking the company too long to collect their money and be able to use it again in the activities of the business. This is not a good sign. The company must figure out how to get the customers to pay them sooner or stop giving them credit at all.

Once you decide that the company is going to survive in the near future, you can turn to estimating its long-term future prospects. As you begin to look beyond the short-term success of a company, the main focus of your attention shifts from information presented on the Balance Sheet to information presented on the Income Statement in order to look at past performance and project any trends into the future.

The long-term future of a company depends, to a very large extent, upon the capability of the company's employees. One of your main goals is to determine how well the employees have done in the past and how well they are doing now. The information that you have already gathered at the beginning of this chapter with regard to the short-term future prospect gives you valuable clues as to current performance. However, this is not sufficient to draw a reliable conclusion about the long-term prospects of the company. chapter 9 will detail how to approach making this sort of evaluation.

GLOSSARY

Average Collection Period: A short-term financial analytical tool calculated by dividing Accounts Receivable by average sales per day. This figure is used by management to determine how long it is taking them to collect their Accounts Receivable. If a company offers payment terms of thirty days to its customers, and the average collection period is longer than thirty days, management needs to determine how to start collecting these receivables faster.

Current Ratio: A short-term financial analytical tool calculated by dividing Current Assets by Current Liabilities. The rule of thumb is that this ratio should be greater than 2.0; however, this will vary somewhat from company to company and industry to industry. Thus, it is necessary to know prior year figures as a basis of comparison.

Inventory Turnover Ratio: A short-term financial analytical tool that is calculated by dividing Cost of Goods Sold by Average Inventory.

(Average Inventory = Beginning Inventory + Ending Inventory/2). What is good or bad for this ratio depends on the industry. If the company is in a business where there are perishable goods, then this number needs to be very low. In a business selling nonperishable goods such as clothes, it would higher. In a business where producing the goods takes a long time—building airplanes, for instance—the ratio would be even higher.

Quick Ratio (or Acid Test Ratio): A short-term financial analytical tool calculated by dividing Quick Assets by Current Liabilities. The rule of thumb for this ratio is that it should be above 1.5. However, as with the current ratio, the history of the company's ratio and the averages in the industry should be considered.

Working Capital: A short-term financial analytical tool calculated by subtracting Current Liabilities from Current Assets. To determine what is a safe and comfortable cushion (sufficient to cover whatever debts may fall due), this figure needs to be compared to the cash flow of the company as well as to prior years' data.

Chapter 9

Using Financial Statements for Long-Term Analysis

- ▶ Quality of Earnings
- ▶ Rate of Return on Investment
- ▶ Sales-Based Ratios or Percentages
- ▶ Earnings Data
- ▶ Long-Term Debt Position
- ▶ Dividend Data
- ▶ Footnotes

Quality of Earnings

In analyzing financial statements, it is important to keep in mind the "quality of earnings" of the company being analyzed. But what is quality of earnings? In general, companies with a high quality of earnings have a strong history of earnings and strong ratios for both the short- and long-terms, and thus are considered to be in a good position to maintain higher earnings in the future. The "quality of earnings" concept is used by both creditors and investors who understand that the bottom line of all organizations is not equal. Companies with higher quality of earnings receive higher credit limits, lower interest costs, and higher stock prices. You can see in Figure 9.1 what produces a higher quality of earnings for a business.

Figure 9.1: WHAT PRODUCES A HIGHER QUALITY OF EARNINGS?

- A majority of Net Income coming from continuing operations as opposed to one-time transactions.
- The quick conversion of sales into cash, i.e., relatively low average collection period
- An appropriate debt-equity ratio
- A fully funded pension Liability
- Stable earning trends
- Highly developed brand loyalty among consumers
- Stable or increasing market share
- An unqualified audit opinion
- Good labor relations

In chapter 8 we reviewed several ratios that are beneficial in analyzing the short-term viability of a company. In Figure 9.2 below, we see that there are also several ratios that need to be reviewed and evaluated to understand the long-term strength of a company. Each of these ratios will be discussed in this chapter.

Figure 9.2: LONG-TERM INFORMATION USED TO EVALUATE A COMPANY

1. Rate of return on investment

2. Net profit as a percentage of sales

3. Percentage of various Expenses to sales

4. Rate of growth of sales

5. Earnings per share

6. Extraordinary gains and losses

7. Price/earnings ratio

8. Number of times interest and preferred stock dividends were earned

9. Total Liabilities to total Assets

10. Dividend payout ratio

Rate of Return on Investment

The rate of return on investment is probably the single most important financial statistic. It comes as close as any figure can to reflecting how well a company has done.

Return on Investment (ROI) is usually calculated as follows:

$$\text{Rate of return (as a ratio)} = \text{Net Income/Average Stockholders' or Owner's Equity}$$

$$\text{Rate of return (as a percentage)} = \text{Net Income/Average Stockholders' or Owner's Equity (x 100)}$$

Note: Stockholders' Equity is the term used in a corporation, whereas, Owner's Equity is the term used in a proprietorship and partnership. They are similar in that they both show how much the owner(s) invested in the business plus their accumulated earnings (Retained Earnings).

This ratio depicts how much money was earned as compared to the amount the owners invested in the business. In the example in chapter 3, Sam had invested $60,000 into the business on January 1. Since the beginning Owner's Equity was $0 on January 1, and the ending Owner's Equity was $70,385 on December 31, the average for the year was $35,193. Since Net Income for 2006 was $10,385, the owner earned 29.5 percent on her investment. ($10,385/$35,193)

Is 29.5 percent a good return on the Owner's Investment? The only way to answer this question is to know what alternative investments an investor might consider. Can the owner invest his money elsewhere and make more money? If the answer is *no*, then the return is a good one. This analysis should be made on an ongoing basis in order to continually determine where to invest one's money.

Having said this, there are exceptions. In the early years of a new company, the owner may not make a great return or any return. But he or she may be "betting" on the future, in the belief that the returns will outpace other alternatives. In addition, a company should consider how well it does in the current year as compared to the previous year by comparing the rate of return figure for each of the two years. Comparing one company's results to those of another company in the same industry is also a useful indicator of how the company is doing in comparison to the competition.

Alert!

Know Your Estimates: In making these comparisons between two years within the same company or between one company and another, you must be alert as to what estimates were made and which generally accepted accounting principles were used. Since Net Income is comprised of several estimates, if these estimates and accounting standards are not the same between years, or between companies, this ratio cannot be compared.

Sales-Based Ratios or Percentages

In order to be able to predict future profitability, you need to examine your company's and other companies' past sales and Expenses.

Net Profit as a Percentage of Sales

One such ratio that aids in the analysis of future profitability is the Net Profit as a percentage of Sales.

Net Profit as a Percentage of Sales = (Net Income/Sales) x 100

An increase in this percentage as compared to previous years may indicate that the company is operating more efficiently. More sales were made with fewer Expenses. Also, when the net profit as a percentage of sales is higher for one company than another, it may indicate that one company has been operating more efficiently than the other.

In the case of the Solana Beach Bicycle Company, Net Income for 2006 was $10,385. Sales for the year were $35,500. Thus, the net profit as a percentage of sales would be 29.25 percent. Is this good? Bad? Helpful? Since this is the first year of operations for the company, we do not have any prior years to compare this number to. However, it does tell us that the company is making over 29 percent on their sales. Not bad. Why? Where else can you invest your money and earn 29 percent? Not very many places, and not on a regular basis. If we had the data we could compare this to other similar small businesses and in the future we will be able to compare it to prior years for the bicycle company. (Once again, keep in mind that the different companies being compared must have used the same GAAP to arrive at their Net Income calculations in order for comparisons to be meaningful.)

Sales Ratios

To help verify these hunches and to gain better insight into operational changes, it is also helpful to compare a variety of different Expenses to the total sales figure. By understanding these ratios of various Expenses to sales, one can determine if a larger or a smaller percentage during the year is being spent on these Expenses. If a company is going to be competitive and successful, it must control its Expenses. These ratios show the areas of the business where the company has been able to control these Expenses. See Figure 9.3 for several examples.

Figure 9.3: **IMPORTANT SALES RATIOS**

1. Cost of goods sold/Sales
2. Selling and delivery Expenses/Sales
3. General and administrative Expenses/Sales
4. Depreciation Expenses/Sales
5. Lease and rental Expenses/Sales
6. Repairs and maintenance Expense/Sales
7. Advertising/Sales
8. Research and development/Sales

Another sales based ratio that is helpful is the rate of growth of sales from one period to the next, calculated by comparing the increase (or decease) in sales between two periods to the sales in the first period. You would find it very informative to learn that Solana Beach Bicycle Company sales increased 10 percent from one year to the next, and 20 percent from year two to three, and 30 percent from year three to four, etc. The pattern of sales over the most recent years of company's life can help you form an estimate of expected future sales.

Earnings Data

The earnings per share figure (EPS) and the price/earnings ratio (P/E) are, along with the rate of return on investment ratio, the most widely used information about corporations. The price/earnings ratio is calculated by dividing the market price per share of that company's stock by the earnings per share of the company.

Price/Earnings Ratio = Market Price Per Share/Earnings Per Share

Alert!

Corporations Only: Both the P/E ratio and Earning Per Share can only be calculated for businesses that have been incorporated. Why? Because if they have not been incorporated, they do not sell capital stock, and therefore, do not have common or preferred shares to perform this calculation. An additional note, if you own a small business that has been incorporated, there may not be a market price for shares. Thus, the P/E ratio cannot be calculated, but EPS can be determined.

The price/earnings ratio can give you some very useful ideas about what other people expect for the future of a company. For example, when a company's stock is selling for fifty times earnings (P/E ratio of fifty to one) and the average P/E ratio for most stocks in that industry is fifteen to one, you may conclude that (1) the company's earnings are going to increase considerably in the future or that (2) the price of the stock is going down between now and the time the present buyers will want to sell the stock.

In general, when the P/E ratio of a company's stock is significantly higher than average, the buyers of the stock expect that the company will prosper; when the ratio is lower than average, buyers are not optimistic about the company's future.

After calculating EPS, you will want to compare the earnings per share figures of a company for a period of five to ten years and should compare the EPS figures with those of other companies.

When looking at Net Income for a company, you must also consider the makeup of that number. Often, there are extraordinary gains or losses included. These are gains/losses from the sale of items that are not considered to be recurring. Since you want to project the past into the future, you want to eliminate from the past data those gains and losses that are not expected to occur again in the future. Therefore, the figure that you will find most useful is the EPS before extraordinary gains and losses when the earnings figure used in the calculation does not include gains or losses that are considered an anomaly or highly unusual in some way. However, you should be sure to look carefully at the extraordinary items and determine the likelihood that they may occur again in the future.

Long-Term Debt Position

Some people believe that a company that borrows money is not as good or as well managed as a company that operates without borrowing. This is not necessarily true. Often, by borrowing money, a company can increase the Net Income for the stockholders without increasing the stockholders' investment.

For example, say that Company A, whose Assets total $100,000, Liabilities total $10,000, and Stockholders' Equity totals $90,000, expects a Net Income next year of $9,000. This represents a return on investment of 10 percent.

Now assume that management is considering the purchase of $40,000 worth of Assets. These Assets will produce additional annual Net Income (before interest Expense) of $4,000. The company has two choices. First it can borrow the $40,000 at 6 percent interest or it can have the investors put the additional $40,000 into the business.

In scenario one, Company A borrows the needed $40,000. Company A's Net Income next year would be $10,600 ($9,000 + $4,000 − $2,400) before Income Taxes. The $2,400 reduction to Net Income is the interest on the loan ($40,000 x 6 percent). Thus, the return on investment would be 11.7 percent ($10,600/$90,000 = 11.7 percent).

In scenario two, instead of borrowing the $40,000, the owners invest their own money. Net income would still increase by $4,000 to $13,000 ($9,000 + $4,000). There would be no interest Expense, and the Return on Stockholders' Equity would be $13,000/$130,000 (the original $90,000 + the additional $40,000). Thus, its Return on investment remains at 10 percent.

As you can see, scenario one, where Company A borrowed the additional $40,000, and ended up with a return on investment of 11.7 percent was a more favorable outcome.

Dangerous Debt: Too much debt can make a company too "risky." During economic downturns, these companies may not be able to repay their debts. However, on the other hand, little or no debt may not be a good thing either. If a company can borrow money at 7 percent interest and earn 10 percent on their investment, borrowing will increase their overall rate of return.

One way to help you determine if a company has put itself into a risky position is to calculate two ratios: the number of times interest was earned and the ratio of total Liabilities to total Assets.

To calculate the number of times that interest was earned, divide the interest Expense into the Net Income before interest Expense and before Income Taxes. You use the income figure before Income Taxes because interest Expense is deductible for Income Tax purposes.

Number of Times Interest Was Earned = Net Income before Interest and Taxes/Interest Expense

The larger this ratio, the easier it is for the company to meet its interest payments, and the less likely it is that the company will default on its loans.

To calculate the ratio of Liabilities to Assets, you divide total Liabilities by total Assets.

Ratio of Liabilities to Assets = Total Liabilities/Total Assets

The idea here is that the larger the ratio, the more risky the company. Of course, a company with a large Liability to Asset ratio may prosper while a company without any debt at all may fail. The Liability to Asset ratio, as well as any ratio, only gives you a part of the total picture and must be analyzed along with other ratios and outside information about the company, the industry, and the economy.

Dividend Data

Additional information about a company can be obtained by looking at the cash dividends that it has paid over the past several years and calculating the dividend payout ratio, the total cash dividends declared during the year divided by the Net Income for the year.

Dividend Payout Ratio = Dividends Declared/Net Income

If the ratio is large, the company is paying out to the stockholders a large portion of the funds earned and not reinvesting them in the company. If this ratio is small or if the company pays no dividends whatsoever, the company may be growing rapidly and using the funds to finance this growth. Which is better? This is completely determined by your personal investment needs if you are a stockholder or the goals of the business if you are part of management.

Figure 9.4 illustrates examples of which long-term ratios are useful for various users.

Figure 9.4: HOW LONG-TERM RATIOS ARE USED

Users	Ratios	Used For
Lenders	Number of Times Interest Was Earned	Evaluating the Safety of Your Loan
	Total Liabilities/ Total Assets	Making Long-Term Loans
Stockholders	EPS, P/E Ratio	Purchasing/Holding Stock
	Dividend Payout Ratio	
Owners/Managers	Sales-Based Ratios	On-Going Long-Term Analysis

Footnotes

Almost all financial statements of companies larger than average small business have footnotes attached to them. The footnotes are as important as the fine print in a contract. When you examine a company's annual report, consider reading the footnotes first. Examine the financial statements next and read the president's message and the rest of the "advertising" last.

Information contained in the footnotes is quite varied. It can include terms of pension plans, terms of stock options outstanding, the nature and expected outcome of any pending lawsuits, terms of a long-term lease agreement, and probable effects of forced sale of properties in a foreign country. You may find an abundance of clues about a company's future from the footnotes.

Analyzing financial statements can be extremely helpful, but without the use of historical data, no predictions could be made about the future of a company. The more you read financial statements, use them, and work with them, the better your decisions about the future of your company and those you wish to invest in will become.

In this chapter you have learned how financial statements and various ratios can be used to evaluate the long-term success of a business In chapter 10 you will learn how to prepare and use a budget.

GLOSSARY

Dividend Payout Ratio: A long-term financial analytical tool calculated by dividing Dividends Declared by Net Income. This ratio is useful when analyzing how much of the earnings for the year have been distributed to the stockholders. As with all other ratios, it must be compared to prior years and to other companies.

Earnings Per Share: A long-term financial analytical tool calculated by dividing Net income by the average number of common shares outstanding for the year. This ratio can only be calculated for corporations. Sometimes this ratio gets too much attention when potential investors are making their decisions. This number is only as accurate and useful as is Net Income itself and must be used in conjunction with many of the other ratios in this chapter.

Extraordinary Gains and Losses: Gains and losses from the sale of items that are neither considered to be recurring nor a normal part of the business operations. For this reason, it is required by GAAP that these gains and losses be separated on the Income Statement from income from operations.

Net Profit as a Percentage of Sales: A long-term financial analytical tool calculated by dividing Net Income by sales and multiplying the results by one hundred. This ratio should be compared with prior year's figures as well as with industry averages to determine its value to management.

Number of Times Interest Was Earned: A long-term financial analytical tool calculated by dividing Net Income before Taxes by interest Expense. The larger this number, the more satisfied the lenders will be since they will have a higher coverage of the interest due to them by the Net Income of the company.

Price/Earnings Ratio: A long-term financial analytical tool calculated by dividing market price per share by earnings per share. This ratio can only be calculated for corporations since partnerships and proprietorships do not have stock and thus have no market price or earnings per share. In general for corporations, the higher this ratio the better, and a positive upward trend in this ratio from year to year is looked on favorably by investors.

Rate of Sales Growth: A long-term financial analytical tool; the percentage change in sales between two or more years. Generally, businesses look for this figure to grow from year to year.

Rate of Return on Investment: A long-term financial analytical tool calculated by dividing Net Income by the average Stockholders' Equity. The average Stockholders' Equity is determined by adding the beginning of the year equity with the end of the year and dividing by two. A good rate of return is one that would be greater than what could be earned investing that money in other places, like with the bank or in bonds or securities.

Chapter 10

Budgeting for Your Business

What Is a Budget?

The budget is a detailed plan that outlines future expectations in quantitative terms. Budgets in accounting can be used for a variety of reasons. You can use a budget to plan and control your future Income and Expenses, which would look like the Income Statements we have been reviewing throughout the book. Or you can use budgets to plan for future capital expenditures, which would show when the company may plan to buy Long-Term Assets and where this money is to come from. Governmental agencies can use budgets of Revenues and Expenses in order to determine their future tax needs.

Planning and Control

So why would Sam want to do a budget for her business? The answer to this question is that Sam is going to produce a budget each year for the purpose of **planning** for her company into the future and to **control** the amount she is spending.

The terms "planning" and "control" are often used interchangeably in an accounting sense, but they are actually two distinct concepts. Planning is the development of future objectives and the preparation of budgets to meet these objectives. Control, on the other hand, involves ensuring that the objectives established during the planning phase are attained. A good budgeting system takes into consideration both the plan and the control.

Advantages of Budgeting

Whether the budget is for personal use or for your business, the major advantage of using a budget is that it gives formality to the planning process. If the budget involves other people, it also serves as a way of communicating the plan to these other people. One of the major processes within an organization is to coordinate and integrate the plans and goals of the various departments. Once the budget has been established it serves as a benchmark for evaluating the actual results.

Without preparing a budget, Sam would not know how much money the bicycle company is going to have at the end of the month, how much it must borrow to buy the capital Assets needed for the business, nor will she know if the Revenues are going to exceed the Expenses or vice versa. The process of preparing the budget will be critical to Sam as she plans for the future. Most small businesses that go out of business do so, not because they don't have a good product or service, but because they have not planned well and have run out of cash. Preparing a budget can help avoid this undesirable end.

QUICK Tip

Using Budgets in Your Business: With the use of personal computers and spreadsheet programs, the budgeting process has been simplified. Budgets can be implemented and maintained at little cost. In addition, it is easy to make changes on a regular basis to view potential situations that may come up. This allows the individual or the manager to more easily make decisions based on these anticipated results, thus implementing the control feature of a budget.

The Master Budget

The master budget is a compilation of many separate budgets that are interdependent. An example of this network is exhibited below in Figure 10.1. The major budgets which together comprise the Master Budget will be the focus of this chapter.

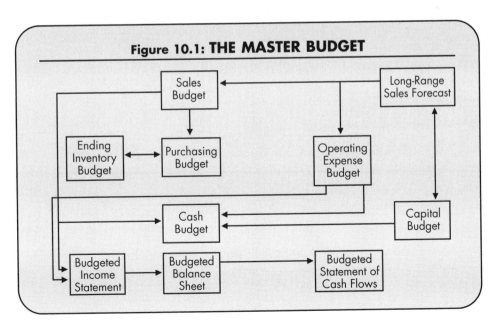

Figure 10.1: THE MASTER BUDGET

Sales Budget

Let's assume that Sam wants to prepare a master budget for the bicycle company for the year 2007. In order to prepare this budget, Sam is going to have to guesstimate how much sales the business will generate for the year. As indicated in Figure 10.1, without this first step of creating a sales budget, none of the other budgets can be prepared.

To calculate the total sales figure, it is necessary to multiply the expected unit sales for each product by its anticipated unit selling price. Sam calculates that total will be $85,000 for anticipated sales of new bicycles. (She expects to sell 170 bicycles at an average price of $500 per bicycle; 170 bicycles x $500 per bicycle = $85,000.)

In addition to the normal sales of bicycles, the bicycle company has been increasing its Revenue from repairs. During 2007, the Revenue from repairs will be budgeted at $9,500. The Expenses associated with these repairs are budgeted to be $3,600.

Cost of Goods Sold and Ending Inventory

Ending Inventory at the end of December 2006 is $13,000. (See Figure 3.2.)

Assume on average, the company has had a 60 percent profit margin. Since sales are budgeted to be $85,000, the Gross Profit would be $51,000 ($85,000 x 60 percent). Further assume that since the company is growing, the bicycle company determines that it wants ending Inventory to grow from the previous year in anticipation of growing sales in the future, so Sam has budgeted ending Inventory for 2007 to be $32,000.

QUICK Tip

Inventory and Budgeting: Determining Inventory needs is not an easy process but is an extremely important one for a small business. Excess Inventory that cannot be sold may become spoiled or out of date. A shortage of Inventory will cause a loss of sales because the product is not available and customers will take their business elsewhere. As a small business owner, careful planning and control is critical to maintaining proper levels of Inventory. This number should be based upon past experiences as well as careful budgeting of sales.

In order for the company to achieve the ending Inventory of $32,000 for 2007, additional Inventory must be purchased. The amount that the company needs to purchase is calculated by the following formula:

Beginning Inventory
+ Purchases
– Ending Inventory
= Cost of Goods Sold

In the case of the bicycle company we know three out of the four numbers:

Beginning Inventory	
(2006 Ending Inventory:	
See Figure 3.3, chapter 3)	$13,000
+ Purchases	???
– Ending Inventory	$32,000
= Cost of Good Sold	$34,000

But wait, how do we know Cost of Goods Sold? Well, we know budgeted sales is $85,000, right? We also know that Gross Profit = $51,000. And lastly, we know that sales – cost of good sold = Gross profit. So voila, $85,000 – X = $51,000. X = $34,000. Whew!

By working backwards, we can calculate that purchases for 2007 must be $53,000.

Operating Expenses

By looking back at the Master Budget in Figure 10.1 we can see that the sales budget flows directly into the budget for operating Expenses. As indicated in Figure 4.1, these Expenses were $7,565, or 21 percent of sales for 2006. Again, assuming that this percentage remains fairly constant and that during the year 2007 sales are budgeted to be $85,000, operating Expenses would be budgeted at $17,850 (21 percent of $85,000).

Capital Budget

The capital budget is concerned with those items that will last longer than one year—the company's Long-Term Assets. To determine if any additional space would need to be rented or built, the business must do a long-range sales forecast. Assuming that the business is growing at a fairly constant rate, Sam has predicted that within two years another building must be purchased in order to meet the business's production and sales demands. Sam's research of local real estate indicates that the cost of a building with sufficient space for the next five years would be $48,000. Therefore, the capital budget per month for the next two years (when the purchase will actually have to be made since Sam does not want to incur any additional debt by taking out a mortgage on this building) would be $2,000. ($48,000/24 months) In order to purchase the building two years from now, $2,000 must be set aside every month for the next two years. (This assumes no inflation during the next two years.)

With the information that has been gathered to this point, it is now possible to create a cash budget and a budgeted Income Statement, Balance Sheet, and cash flow. Let's examine this information.

Budgeted Income Statement

Using the figures calculated above, Sam can create a budgeted Income Statement like the one shown in Figure 10.2:

Figure 10.2: SOLANA BEACH BICYCLE COMPANY
Budgeted Income Statement
For the Year Ended December 31, 2007

Sales	$85,000
Cost of Goods Sold	34,000
Gross Profit	$51,000
Operating Expenses	17,850
Net Income from Operations	$33,150

Other Revenue:

Repair Revenue	$9,500

Other Expenses:

Repair Expenses 3,600

Net Income $39,050

Why does the bicycle company need this Income Statement? They might use it to show to the bank to get a loan. They might want to show it to potential partners looking for information about the future of the business. And of course, they will also need it for planning how they are going to expand in the future!

The Cash Budget

Next, the company needs to calculate how much cash they are going to have at the end of the year. Sam needs to know this figure in order to prepare the budgeted Balance Sheet, but more importantly, to make sure the company has enough cash to pay its bills in the following periods, and keep the cash balance at a "safe level."

In order to calculate the budgeted ending cash balance for 2007 we need to know the beginning cash balance. This figure is the same as the ending cash balance on December 31, 2006, because the business starts the new year with the amount of cash it ended the last year with. This figure is $17,385 (see Figure 3.2). A number of assumptions need to be made as well. Sales for 2007 were predicted to be $85,000 plus $9,500 for repairs (for a total of $94,500), but it must also be determined how much of these sales will be in cash and how much will be on Accounts Receivable. In the past, 75 percent of both the bicycle sales and repair work have been paid for with cash, so it is safe to assume that this will be the case for 2007 as well. Thus, the cash receipts for 2007 from sales and repairs will be $70,875 ($94,500 x 75 percent).

Assuming the same ratio applies to the preceding year (that is, 75 percent of the sales were for cash, and the other 25 percent were on account) then the 25 percent that was still owed to the bicycle company on December 31, 2006, will be collected in 2007. This is making the assumption that there were no bad debts. (If there were bad debts, then the amount estimated for bad debts would be deducted from the amount to be collected.) Again, since the sales and the repair work for 2006 totaled $39,350, the cash to be collected in 2007 on these 2006 sales would be $9,837 ($39,350 x 25 percent).

Now we need to calculate the cash expenditures for 2007. The first expenditure is that of purchasing Inventory. The general rule at Solana Beach Bicycle Company is that 80 percent of the purchase is paid in cash in the year of purchase, and 20 percent is paid in the following year. In 2006, the bicycle company purchased $23,000 of bicycles (Inventory) and in 2007, they purchased bicycles costing $53,000. Thus, the cash expenditure for 2007 is $47,000. (20 percent of $23,000 for 2006 and 80 percent of $53,000 for 2007).

So continuing with this assumption, 80 percent of the other expenditures at Solana Beach Bicycle Company are paid with cash in the year of use, and 20 percent are charged on account. (Every company will have its own past data to guide their assumptions for the purposes of preparing budgets and will calculate this ratio (80/20, 65/35, etc.) based upon its own experiences.) Operating Expenses for 2007 have been budgeted at $17,850, and operating Expenses in 2006 totaled $7,565 (See Figure 4.1). Based on the 80/20 breakdown of cash versus account payment at Solana Beach Bicycle Company, we know that the total cash outlay for operating Expenses in 2007 would be $15,793: the sum of the cash outlay for 2007 expenditures ($17,850 x 80 percent = $14,280) plus the cash spent to settle Accounts Payable for 2006 operating Expenses ($7,565 x 20 percent = $1,513).

Each year, another cash expenditure is made for repair Expenses. All of these expenditures are made in the year in which they occur. Thus, the $3,600 for repairs in 2007 are all paid in the year 2007.

The last cash "expenditure" that the bicycle company made during 2007 is the $2,000 per month that the business "put aside" for the future purchase of a building. This cash transaction is neither an expenditure nor a reduction in cash. It is simply going from one bank account to another. The only reason for the transaction at all is to make sure that the cash left in the operating cash account is not accidentally spent prior to the purchase of the building.

Let's take a look below at Figure 10.3 to see how we can actually calculate the ending cash balance.

Figure 10.3: SOLANA BEACH BICYCLE COMPANY
Budgeted Ending Cash Balance
For the Year Ended December 31, 2007

Beginning Cash	$17,385
Add:	
Cash Receipts from 2007 Sales	70,875
Cash Receipts from 2006 Sales	9,837
Subtract:	
Cash Payments for Inventory Purchases 2007	42,400
Cash Payments for Inventory Purchases 2006	4,600
Cash Payments for Operating Expenses in 2007	14,280
Cash Payments for Operating Expenses in 2006	1,513
Cash Payments for Repairs Expenses in 2007	3,600
Ending Cash Balance	$31,704

(Note to the Cash Budget: Of the $31,704 ending cash balance, $24,000 has been set aside in a separate bank account for the future purchase of a new building.)

The example presented here is for a small business such as Solana Beach Bicycle Company. However, the same concepts can be applied to preparing a personal budget and the same benefits will be derived.

QUICK Tip

Participation Is Key: The success or failure of budgets within an organization is usually enhanced by the participation of the managers, who are generally more apt to fulfill the goals that they have had a direct role in developing. This isn't to say that these budgets should not be subject to review by higher management; however, any changes that are made should be done with the involvement of the individuals who played a part in creating the budget.

In this chapter you learned the meaning of a budget, the value of preparing one, and the ways in which the components interrelate. In chapter 11 you will find out who auditors are, what type of reports they issue, and why those reports are useful to you.

GLOSSARY

Budget: A detailed plan that outlines future expectations in quantitative terms. The major purposes of a budget are to plan for the future and to control the operations of the company. The budget is prepared on an ongoing basis and adjusted continually with the acquisition of additional information.

Capital Budget: The budget for Long-Term Assets. Not only does this budget help determine what future capital (long-term) Assets are needed for the business, but also how much money needs to be set aside each month or quarter to acquire these Assets in the future.

Control: Involves ensuring that the objectives established during the planning phase of the budget preparation are attained. For example, once it is determined that the amount of cash needed at the end of the year is $40,000, all during the year the cash account needs to be monitored by careful review of the budget and decisions made to ensure the desired ending balance is attained.

Master Budget: A network of many separate budgets that are interdependent. The master budget starts with the Sales Budget. Once it is estimated how much in sales is going to occur during the year, all of the other budgets for Inventory, purchases, cash, and Expenses, et al, can be determined.

Planning: The development of future objectives and the preparation of budgets to meet those objectives. Without a budget, there is no planning, and companies that attempt to operate their businesses without this type of planning base their success on luck.

Chapter 11

Audits and Auditors

What Is an Audit?

One of the rules that the Securities Exchange Commission (SEC) has issued is that the financial statements of public companies (those companies selling stock to the public) must be examined by an independent public accountant through the process of an audit. This rule means that an accountant, who is not an employee of the company and who is licensed to practice as a public accountant by the state where the financial statements are being prepared, must audit (or examine) the records of the company and must determine whether or not the financial statements are in accordance with the rules of Generally Accepted Accounting Principles (GAAP). In addition, the auditor has the responsibility to give reasonable assurance that the financial statements are free of any material misstatement.

The American Accounting Association defines auditing as "a systematic process of objectively obtaining and evaluating evidence regarding assertions about economic actions and events to ascertain the degree of correspondence between those assertions and established criteria and communicating the results to interested users." (From American Accounting Association Committee on Basic Auditing Concepts, A Statement of Basic Auditing Concepts; Sarasota, FL, American Accounting Association, 1973.)

When auditors issue their reports they must follow a set of rules known as Generally Accepted Auditing Standards (GAAS). These standards are made up of 1) the ten Generally Accepted Auditing Standards, 2) the Statements on Auditing Standards (SASs), and 3) the Interpretations of these Standards.

These standards have been the jurisdiction of the American Institute of Certified Public Accountants and their Auditing Standards Board. With the passage of the Sarbanes-Oxley Act of 2002, Congress has now taken the responsibility for creating standards for public companies and created the Public Company Accounting Oversight Board (PCAOB) for this purpose. The board has the additional responsibility to make sure that audit quality is not compromised and that auditor performance meets public expectations.

In addition to the auditing standards, CPAs are expected to follow the Code of Ethics established by the profession. By establishing and adhering to such a code, this ensures the auditor's independence—the major attribute the auditor has to sell to the public.

A typical auditor's report (known as the unqualified report) is issued when the financial statements are in accordance with GAAP. This report is written and issued by the auditors and is submitted to the public with the financial statements.

 Remember that the financial statements are prepared by and are the responsibility of the management of the company and not the auditors. Since the major corporate failures of the 1990s and early 2000s, the Sarbanes-Oxley Act of 2002 requires company management to sign a letter stating that the financial statements are presented fairly in accordance with Generally Accepted Accounting Principles, just as the auditors must.

Accounting Versus Auditing

As we have discussed in previous chapters, accounting is the process of recording, classifying, and summarizing economic events in a process that leads to the preparation of financial statements.

Auditing, on the other hand, is not concerned with the preparation of the accounting data, but with the evaluation of this data to determine if it is properly presented in accordance with the rules of accounting (GAAP) and whether it properly reflects the events that have occurred during the period in question.

Types of Auditors

An auditor is an individual who checks the accuracy and fairness of the accounting records of a company and determines whether the financial statements are in accordance with the Generally Accepted Accounting Principles. Three different types of auditors are described below.

The Certified Public Accountant (CPA)

Certified Public Accountants (CPAs) are auditors who serve the needs of the general public by providing auditing, tax planning and preparation, and management consulting services. CPAs can work as individuals or as employees of a firm; these firms range in size from one individual to international partnerships with more than two thousand partners.

The largest of these firms have offices worldwide and are referred to as the "Big Four." Even though they only employ about 12 percent of all of the CPAs in the United States, they actually perform the audits of about 85 percent of the largest corporations in the world. These four companies are: Deloitte & Touche, Ernst & Young, KPMG, and PricewaterhouseCoopers.

Those individuals who act as independent auditors must be licensed to perform audits by the state in which they practice. The laws vary from state to state as to the requirements that must be met in order to obtain such licenses. However, to be issued a license to practice as a CPA, all states require the individual to pass a uniform examination, which is prepared and graded by the American Institute of CPAs (AICPA). In addition to passing this examination, most states require an individual to have some experience working with another CPA prior to being licensed. Most states also require that after being licensed to practice as a public accountant, CPAs must take at least a certain minimum amount of continuing education coursework each year in order to have their license renewed.

Internal Auditors

Internal auditors are employed by companies to audit the companies' own records and to establish a system of internal control. The functions of these auditors vary greatly, depending upon the needs and expectations of management. In general, the work includes compliance audits (to make sure the accounting is in compliance with the rules of the company and the laws under which they operate) and operational audits (a review of an organization's operating procedures for efficiency and effectiveness). Operational Audits review the business for efficient use of resources; they are meant to help management make decisions that will make the company more profitable.

As with CPAs, many internal auditors are also certified by passing a nationally prepared examination. This examination is for the Certificate of Internal Auditing and is prepared by the Institute of Internal Auditors.

Internal auditors generally must report to the highest level of responsibility within the company; this may include the Board of Directors or the Audit Committee of the Board of Directors. This is important because it gives the internal auditors more independence from the management team that they are reporting on.

During a company's audit, internal auditors work closely with whatever external auditors (CPAs) have been hired by the company in order to reduce the amount of time that the outside auditor needs to spend with the company. Given the size of the internal audit staff and their independence within the company, they may be asked to perform several of the tasks that would have been prepared by the external auditors. The external auditors still have the ultimate responsibility to determine if the financial statements are presented in accordance with Generally Accepted Accounting Principles, and they are the ones who sign the report that is presented to the public. Using internal auditors is simply meant to reduce the number of detailed procedures that would otherwise have to be performed by the external auditors.

Governmental Auditors

As you would expect, governmental auditors are individuals who perform the audit function within or on behalf of a governmental organization. As with the other two types of auditors described above, these individuals also must be independent from the individuals or groups that they are auditing.

The different governmental organizations that most commonly hire and use auditors include the United States General Accounting Office (GAO). The major function of this group is to perform the audit function for Congress. The Internal Revenue Service hires auditors to enforce the federal tax laws as defined by the Congress and interpreted by the courts. Several other governmental organizations hire auditors to ensure that the regulations affecting those entities under their jurisdictions are met. Some of these include: the Bureau of Alcohol, Tobacco, and Firearms (ATF), the Drug Enforcement Agency (DEA), and the Federal Bureau of Investigation (FBI). Rather than following Generally Accepted Accounting Principles, government audits are done in accordance with a set of accounting rules established by the Governmental Accounting Standards Board (GASB).

The Standard Audit Opinion Illustrated

The most common document issued by auditors as part of their reports is the standard unqualified audit opinion. It is issued under the following situations:

1. All financial statements have been examined by the auditor.
2. It is determined that these financial statements were prepared in accordance with GAAP.
3. The auditor has gathered sufficient evidence to give an opinion on these statements.
4. The auditor is independent of the company being audited.
5. The auditor has followed the generally accepted rules of auditing called Generally Accepted Auditing Standards (GAAS).

The Generally Accepted Auditing Standards that auditors must follow are spelled out in the rules of the auditing profession in a set of standards that is always changing. The rules come from two sources, the AICPA and the SEC. With the standards always changing, this provides an example of how the SEC and the AICPA complement and support each other to help ensure that the financial statements issued to the public present useful information that is relevant, reliable, understandable, and sufficient for use in making decisions about firms and their management.

When all of these conditions are met, a report like the one in Figure 11.1 below will be issued. Notice that the report is issued on a comparative basis, and therefore the management of the company must attach two years' of financial statements.

The report has three basic segments: 1) the introductory paragraph, 2) the scope paragraph, and 3) the opinion paragraph.

Figure 11.1: **THE UNQUALIFIED AUDIT OPINION (STANDARD)**

Sydney and Maude
Certified Public Accountants
7 Circle Drive
Cape Cod, MA 02117

Report of Independent Registered Public Accounting Firm

To: the Board of Directors and Shareholders, The Las Brisas Company

We have audited the accompanying Balance Sheets of The Las Brisas Company as of December 31, 2006, and 2005, and the related statements of income, shareholders' equity, and cash flows for the years then ended. These financial statements are the responsibility of the Company's management. Our responsibility is to express an opinion on these financial statements based on our audits.

We conducted our audits in accordance with auditing standards of the Public Company Accounting Oversight Board. Those standards require that we plan and perform the audit to obtain reasonable assurance about whether the financial statements are free of material misstatement. An audit includes examining, on a test basis, evidence supporting the amounts and disclosures in the financial statements. An audit also includes assessing the accounting principles used and significant estimates made by management, as well as evaluating the overall financial statement presentation. We believe that our audits provide a reasonable basis for our opinion.

In our opinion, the financial statements referred to above present fairly, in all material respects, the financial position of the Las Brisas Company as of December 31, 2006, and 2005 and the results of its operations and its cash flows for the years then ended in conformity with accounting principles generally accepted in the United States.

Sydney and Maude, CPAs

Cape Cod, Massachusetts

March 17, 2007

See Appendix B for the audit option in the Station Casinos Annual Report.

The Parts of the Report

There are seven parts to every standard audit report. They include:

Figure 11.2: **STANDARD AUDIT REPORT**

1. The report title—"Independent Auditor's Report"

2. The audit report address—"To the Stockholder's..."

3. Introductory paragraph—"We have audited..."

4. Scope paragraph—"We conducted our audits..."

5. Opinion paragraph—"In our opinion..."

6. Signature of CPA firm—"Sydney and Maude, CPAs"

7. Audit report date—"March 17, 2007. This date represents when the work on the audit was completed, not the date the report was issued. Depending on the size of the company being audited, the review of the evidence may take two to three months.

The wording on this report may vary slightly from auditor to auditor; however, the overall structure and meaning remain the same.

Other Types of Audit Reports

Below is a brief overview of three other types of audit reports that you might encounter when reviewing financial statements and with which you should be familiar.

A qualified audit report is issued by the auditor when they conclude that the financial statements are presented in accordance with GAAP, except for some specified items being different.

An adverse audit report is issued by auditors when they conclude that the financial statements are not presented fairly in accordance with the rules of accounting (GAAP).

A disclaimer audit report is issued by auditors when they do not have enough information to determine whether the financial statements are in accordance with the accounting rules. Auditors would also issue this type of report if they were not independent of the company being audited.

Why Audits Are Useful to You

As the business world becomes more global and complex, so do the financial reports that companies issue. The information provided and the rules that govern their presentation have exploded in number and complexity during the past twenty years. Today it is becoming more and more difficult for the layperson (non-accountants) to fully understand these presentations. The auditor's report of a company's financial statements gives the reader and user of these financial statements an assurance that this information is in accordance with an established set of rules (GAAP) and reviewed by the auditor who is independent of management.

The use of an independent audit can generally assure the user that the information contained in a company's financial statements is free of material errors and fraud. This assurance supports the user in making investment and analytical decisions about the company being reviewed.

Alert!

Audits Have Their Limits: These audits do not guarantee the dollar accuracy or predictive ability of these financial statements. It only guarantees that they are presented in accordance with a set of accounting rules (GAAP). Many people believe that the auditor will either stop or detect all fraud within an organization, but this is not necessarily the case. Even though auditors do follow procedures that help detect fraud, they cannot detect or disclose all such instances.

GLOSSARY

"Big Four" Accounting Firms: The four largest CPA firms in the world with offices worldwide. PricewaterhouseCoopers, KPMG, Deloitt & Touche, and Ernst & Young perform the audits of the majority of the world's large companies.

Adverse Audit Report: A type of report issued by a CPA firm at the completion of an audit. This report is issued when the CPA concludes that the financial statements being audited are not in accordance with Generally Accepted Accounting Principles.

Audit: The accumulation and evaluation of evidence about a company's financial statements to determine if they are in accordance with GAAP.

Auditor: The individual who checks the accuracy and fairness of the accounting records of a company and issues a report as to whether the company's financial records are in accordance with Generally Accepted Accounting Principles.

Certified Public Accountant (CPA): Auditors who serve the needs of the general public. These individuals have passed an examination, in most cases have 150 hours of college credits, have worked with another CPA for a minimum of two years, and complete a required twenty to forty hours of continuing education each year. Their work includes auditing, tax planning and preparation, and management consulting.

Compliance Audits: An audit that makes sure the accounting is in compliance with the rules being reviewed. Most often these types of audits are governmental audits, in that they determine whether the financial statements are in compliance with government regulations. They can, however, also be used to check compliance in other instances, such as when a bank requires certain stipulations be met in order for a company to receive or to continue with a loan.

Disclaimer Audit Report: A type of report issued by a CPA firm at the completion of an audit. This report is issued when the CPA concludes that he or she does not have enough information to determine whether the financial statements are or are not in accordance with the accounting rules.

Governmental Auditors: The individuals who perform the audit function for a governmental organization such as the U.S. General Accounting Office (GAO), the Internal Revenue Service (IRS), the Securities and Exchange Commission (SEC), Bureau of Alcohol, Tobacco, and Firearms (ATF), Drug Enforcement Agency (DEA), and the Federal Bureau of Investigation (FBI), as well as state and local governments.

Rather than following Generally Accepted Accounting Principles, government audits are done in accordance with a set of accounting rules established by the Governmental Accounting Standards Board (GASB).

Internal auditors: These auditors are employed by companies to audit the company's own records. These individuals are not necessarily certified public accountants (CPAs), but many are certified internal auditors (CIA). To ensure autonomy, these individuals report directly to the audit committee or board of directors of the company rather than to company management.

Operational Audit: A review of an organization's operating procedures for the purpose of making recommendations about the efficiency and effectiveness of business objectives and compliance with company policy. The goal of this type of an audit is to help managers discharge their responsibilities and maximize profitability.

Qualified Audit Report: A type of report issued by a CPA firm at the completion of an audit. This report is issued when the CPA concludes that the financial statements being audited are presented in accordance with GAAP, except for some specified items being different; for example, the use of a nonstandard type of Inventory evaluation is used.

Public Company Accounting Oversight Board (PCAOB): Established by Congress as part of the Sarbanes-Oxley Law of 2002, the PCAOB is charged with the responsibility of creating accounting standards for public companies. The Board has the additional responsibility to make sure that audit quality is not compromised and that auditor performance meets public expectations.

Unqualified Audit Report: A type of report issued by a CPA firm at the completion of an audit. This report is issued when the CPA concludes that the financial statements being audited are completely in accordance with Generally Accepted Accounting Principles.

Appendix

Internet for Accountants

What Resources Are Available for Accountants?

The amount of information available to accountants and other professionals in business continues to grow each day. In the past, accessing this information was extremely burdensome and time-consuming, but the advent of computers and the Internet have placed an abundance of information at your fingertips.

The Internet has also changed the way in which accountants and auditors do their work. Financial reporting, financial information systems, practices in auditing, management and control, tax accounting, and forensic accounting have all been changed for the better by the

Internet. Without understanding the power of the Internet, an accountant is at a loss to access the wealth of information that is available.

The listing below is only partial and does not cover all topics of interest to accountants. However, part of the fun of being on the Internet is "surfing the Web" to find the links that are most interesting to you and to your particular interests. Here are some sites to get you started:

The IRS Homepage
http://www.irs.ustreas.gov

The National Association of Enrolled Agents
http://www.naea.org

The American Institute of Certified Public Accountants
http://www.aicpa.org/index.htm

The American Accounting Association
http://www.aaahq.org

The Financial Accounting Standards Board
http://www.fasb.org

The Association of Government Accountants
http://www.agacgfm.org

The Governmental Accounting Standards Board
http://www.gasb.org

The Institute of Internal Auditors
http://www.theiia.org

The Institute of Management Accountants
http://www.imanet.org

The Association of Certified Fraud Examiners
http://www.acfe.com

The International Accounting Standards Board
http://www.iasb.org

State Accounting Societies and Boards
http://www.aicpa.org/states/index.htm

A Listing of CPA Firms
http://www.cpafirms.com

The Sarbanes-Oxley Act Explained
http://sarbanes-oxley.com

Free Annual Reports
http://ftcom.ar.wilink.com

Access to Free Audit Programs
http://www.auditnet.org

Top 10 Accounting Software Programs
http://www.2020software.com

Glossary of Accounting Terms
http://www.accountz.com/glossary.html

Top 50 Overlooked Tax Deductions
http://www.jacksonhewitt.com/resources_library_top50.asp

Corporate SEC Filings
http://edgar-online.com

Financial Calculators

http://www.bcscpa.com/calcs/index.htm
http://www.fool.com/calcs/calculators.htm?source=LN

Stock Quotes

http://quotes.nasdaq.com/asp/MasterDataEntry.asp?page=flashQuotes

Newspapers

New York Times (http://www.nytimes.com)
Wall Street Journal (http://wsj.com)

Once again, this is just a starter list. Have fun surfing the net!

Appendix B

Financial Statements— Station Casinos, Inc.

The financial statements contained here are from the actual 2004 annual report of Station Casinos, Inc., a Las Vegas-based company which operates several casinos and hotels in the Las Vegas, Nevada, area. They will give you an excellent idea of what these statements look like for major corporations.

MANAGEMENT'S DISCUSSION AND ANALYSIS OF
FINANCIAL CONDITION AND RESULTS OF OPERATIONS

The following discussion and analysis should be read in conjunction with "Selected Consolidated Financial Data"
and the financial statements and notes thereto included elsewhere in this Annual Report.

RESULTS OF OPERATIONS

The following table highlights the results of our operations (dollars in thousands):

	Year ended December 31, 2004	Percent change	Year ended December 31, 2003	Percent change	Year ended December 31, 2002
Net revenues – total	$ 986,742	15.0 %	$ 858,089	8.2 %	$ 792,865
Major Las Vegas Operations (a)	868,248	11.2 %	781,061	1.6 %	768,813
Management fees (b)	84,618	81.2 %	46,711	862.5 %	4,853
Other Operations and Corporate (c)	33,876	11.7 %	30,317	57.9 %	19,199
Operating income (loss) – total	$ 257,055	82.2 %	$ 141,071	(3.3)%	$ 145,910
Major Las Vegas Operations (a)	232,678	36.4 %	170,566	(7.9)%	185,170
Management fees (b)	84,618	81.2 %	46,711	862.5 %	4,853
Other Operations and Corporate (c)	(60,241)	20.9 %	(76,206)	(72.8)%	(44,113)
Cash flows provided by (used in)					
Operating activities	$ 261,596	33.2 %	$ 196,451	47.8 %	$ 132,898
Investing activities	(337,114)	(82.9)%	(184,317)	(205.2)%	(60,393)
Financing activities	81,663	987.5 %	(9,201)	88.4 %	(79,283)

(a) Includes the wholly owned properties of Palace Station, Boulder Station, Texas Station, Sunset Station, Santa Fe Station, Fiesta Rancho and Fiesta Henderson.

(b) Includes management fees from Thunder Valley (since June 9, 2003), Green Valley Ranch Station and Barley's.

(c) Includes the wholly owned properties of Wild Wild West, Wildfire (since January 27, 2003), Magic Star (since August 2, 2004), Gold Rush (since August 2, 2004), and Corporate and Development expense.

Net Revenues
Consolidated net revenues for the year ended December 31, 2004 increased 15.0% to $986.7 million as compared to $858.1 million for the year ended December 31, 2003. The increase in consolidated net revenues was due to an $81.9 million increase in casino revenues and an increase in management fees from Thunder Valley, which includes a full year of operations. Net revenues increased primarily due to a strong Las Vegas local economy, continued population and employment growth in the Las Vegas valley, no new competition in the local's market, as well as the continued success of our Jumbo brand products, including Jumbo Jackpot. Jumbo Jackpot, which we introduced in April 2003, is an exclusive progressive slot jackpot that allows customers using a Boarding Pass or Amigo Club card the opportunity to win between $50,000 and $150,000 just for playing slot machines.

Consolidated net revenues for the year ended December 31, 2003 increased 8.2% to $858.1 million as compared to $792.9 million for the year ended December 31, 2002. The increase in consolidated net revenues was primarily due to management and development fees from Thunder Valley, which opened on June 9, 2003. Overall population growth in the Las Vegas valley, as well as the introduction of Jumbo Jackpot in April 2003, were also contributing factors to the increase in consolidated net revenues.

Operating Income/Operating Margin

In analyzing year-to-year comparative operating results, management takes into consideration the effect of certain charges and credits on operating income. The following table identifies these charges and credits and the resulting operating income and operating margins, excluding such charges and credits (dollars in thousands):

| | *Years ended December 31,* | | |
	2004	2003	2002
Operating income	$ 257,055	$ 141,071	$ 145,910
Operating margin	26.1%	16.4%	18.4%
Certain charges/credits:			
Thunder Valley development fee	–	(4,595)	–
Impairment loss	–	18,868	8,791
Litigation settlement	–	38,000	–
Preopening expenses	848	–	–
Operating income, excluding certain charges/credits	$ 257,903	$ 193,344	$ 154,701
Operating margin, excluding certain charges/credits	26.1%	22.5%	19.5%

Consolidated operating income, excluding certain charges/credits, increased 33.4% in the year ended December 31, 2004 as compared to the year ended December 31, 2003. This increase is primarily due to increased consolidated net revenues noted above. There is significant operating leverage on incremental revenue due to a significant amount of fixed costs. As a result, our consolidated operating margin, excluding certain charges/credits, improved 3.6 percentage points in the year ended December 31, 2004 as compared to the year ended December 31, 2003.

Consolidated operating income, excluding certain charges/credits, increased 25.0% in the year ended December 31, 2003 as compared to the year ended December 31, 2002. This increase is primarily due to management fees from Thunder Valley, which opened on June 9, 2003. As a result, our consolidated margin, excluding certain charges/credits, improved 3.0 percentage points in the year ended December 31, 2003 as compared to the year ended December 31, 2002.

The following table highlights our various sources of revenues and expenses as compared to prior years (dollars in thousands):

	Year ended December 31, 2004	Percent change	Year ended December 31, 2003	Percent change	Year ended December 31, 2002
Casino revenues	$ 730,584	12.6 %	$ 648,664	1.7 %	$ 638,113
Casino expenses	273,816	3.2 %	265,203	2.6 %	258,383
Margin	62.5%		59.1%		59.5%
Food and beverage revenues	$ 140,332	5.0 %	$ 133,676	(0.1)%	$ 133,811
Food and beverage expenses	100,548	14.5 %	87,783	11.5 %	78,738
Margin	28.4%		34.3%		41.2%
Room revenues	$ 57,057	13.1 %	$ 50,460	3.9 %	$ 48,579
Room expenses	21,053	7.5 %	19,580	3.1 %	19,000
Margin	63.1%		61.2%		60.9%
Other revenues	$ 42,008	(8.6) %	$ 45,943	12.6 %	$ 40,790
Other expenses	16,820	8.9 %	15,452	(5.1)%	16,276
Management fees	$ 84,618	81.2 %	$ 46,711	862.5 %	$ 4,853
Selling, general and administrative expenses	$ 172,923	7.0 %	$ 161,643	0.4 %	$ 161,038
Percent of net revenues	17.5%		18.8%		20.3%
Corporate expense	$ 47,189	42.8 %	$ 33,039	3.4 %	$ 31,946
Percent of net revenues	4.8%		3.9%		4.0%
Earnings from joint ventures	$ 26,524	28.7 %	$ 20,604	82.4 %	$ 11,293

CRITICAL ACCOUNTING POLICIES

Significant Accounting Policies and Estimates

We prepare our consolidated financial statements in conformity with accounting principles generally accepted in the United States. Certain of our accounting policies, including the determination of slot club program liability, the estimated useful lives assigned to our assets, asset impairment, insurance reserves, purchase price allocations made in connection with our acquisitions and the calculation of our income tax liabilities, require that we apply significant judgment in defining the appropriate assumptions for calculating financial estimates. By their nature, these judgments are subject to an inherent degree of uncertainty. Our judgments are based on our historical experience, terms of existing contracts, observance of trends in the gaming industry and information available from other outside sources. There can be no assurance that actual results will not differ from our estimates. To provide an understanding of the methodology we apply, our significant accounting policies and basis of presentation are discussed below, as well as where appropriate in this discussion and analysis and in the notes to our consolidated financial statements.

Slot Club Programs

Our Boarding Pass and Amigo Club player rewards programs (the "Programs") allow customers to redeem points earned from their gaming activity at all Station and Fiesta properties for complimentary food, beverage, rooms, entertainment and merchandise. At the time redeemed, the retail value of complimentaries under the Programs are recorded as revenue with a corresponding offsetting amount included in promotional allowances. The cost associated with complimentary food, beverage, rooms, entertainment and merchandise redeemed under the Programs is recorded in casino costs and expenses. We also record a liability for the estimated cost of the outstanding points under the Programs.

Self-Insurance Reserves

We are self insured up to certain stop loss amounts for workers' compensation, major medical and general liability costs. Insurance claims and reserves include accruals of estimated settlements for known claims, as well as accruals of estimates for claims incurred but not reported. In estimating these accruals, we consider historical loss experience and make judgments about the expected levels of costs per claim. We believe our estimates of future liability are reasonable based upon our methodology; however, changes in health care costs, accident frequency and severity and other factors could materially affect the estimate for these liabilities.

Derivative Instruments

We enter into interest rate swaps from time to time in order to manage interest rate risks associated with our current and anticipated future borrowings. The interest rate swaps that we have entered into qualify for the "shortcut" method allowed under SFAS No. 133, "Accounting for Derivative Instruments and Hedging Activities" (and as amended by SFAS No. 138), which allows for an assumption of no ineffectiveness. As such, there is no income statement impact from changes in the fair value of the hedging instruments. Instead, the fair value of the instrument is recorded as an asset or liability on our balance sheet with an offsetting adjustment to the carrying value of the related debt.

Property and Equipment

Property and equipment are stated at cost. Depreciation and amortization are computed using the straight-line method over the estimated useful lives of the assets or the terms of the capitalized lease, whichever is less. Costs of major improvements are capitalized, while costs of normal repairs and maintenance are charged to expense as incurred.

We evaluate our property and equipment and other long-lived assets for impairment in accordance with SFAS No. 144, "Accounting for the Impairment or Disposal of Long-Lived Assets". For assets to be disposed of, we recognize the asset to be sold at the lower of carrying value or fair market value less costs of disposal. Fair market value for assets to be disposed of is generally estimated based on comparable asset sales, solicited offers or a discounted cash flow model. For assets to be held and used, we review fixed assets for impairment whenever indicators of impairment exist. If an indicator of impairment exists, we compare the estimated future cash flows of the asset, on an undiscounted basis, to the carrying value of the asset. If the undiscounted cash flows exceed the carrying value, no impairment is indicated. If the undiscounted cash flows do not exceed the carrying value, then impairment is measured based on fair value compared to carrying value, with fair value typically based on a discounted cash flow model. Our consolidated financial statements reflect all adjustments required by SFAS No. 144 as of December 31, 2004.

Goodwill and Other Intangibles

The FASB issued SFAS No. 142, "Goodwill and Other Intangible Assets", in June 2001. SFAS No. 142 changed the accounting for goodwill from an amortization method to an impairment-only approach. Amortization of goodwill, including goodwill recorded in past business combinations, ceased upon the adoption of SFAS No. 142. We implemented SFAS No. 142 on January 1, 2002 and tested for impairment in accordance with the provisions of SFAS No. 142 in the first quarter of 2002 and annually perform such test. In order to test for impairment of goodwill, we use the Income Approach, which focuses on the income-producing capability of the respective property. The underlying premise of this approach is that the value of an asset can be measured by the present worth of the net economic benefit (cash receipts less cash outlays) to be received over the life of the subject asset. The steps followed in applying this approach include estimating the expected after-tax cash flows attributable to the respective property and converting these after-tax cash flows to present value through discounting. The discounting process uses a rate of return, which accounts for both the time value of money and investment risk factors. The present value of the after-tax cash flows is then totaled to arrive at an indication of the fair value of the goodwill. If the fair value of the goodwill exceeds the carrying value, then impairment is measured based on the difference between the calculated fair value and the carrying value. Our consolidated financial statements reflect all adjustments required by SFAS No. 142 as of December 31, 2004.

Income Taxes

We are subject to income taxes in the United States of America and file a consolidated federal income tax return. We account for income taxes according to SFAS No. 109, "Accounting for Income Taxes". SFAS No. 109 requires the recognition of deferred tax assets, net of applicable reserves, related to net operating loss carry forwards and certain temporary differences. A valuation allowance is recognized if, based on the weight of available evidence, it is more likely than not that some portion or all of the deferred tax asset will not be recognized.

Our income tax returns are subject to examination by the Internal Revenue Service and other tax authorities. We regularly assess the potential outcomes of these examinations in determining the adequacy of our provision for income taxes and our income tax liabilities. Inherent in our determination of any necessary reserves are assumptions based on past experiences and judgments about potential actions by taxing authorities. Our estimate of the potential outcome for any uncertain tax issue is highly judgmental. We believe that we have adequately provided for any reasonable and foreseeable outcome related to uncertain tax matters.

Recently Issued Accounting Standards

In December 2004, the FASB issued Statement of Financial Accounting Standards No. 123R (Revised 2004), "Share-Based Payment" ("SFAS No. 123R"), which requires that the compensation cost relating to share-based payment transactions be recognized in financial statements based on alternative fair value models. The share-based compensation cost will be measured based on fair value models of the equity or liability instruments issued. We currently disclose pro forma compensation expense quarterly and annually by calculating the stock option grants' fair value using the Black-Scholes model and disclosing the impact on net income and net income per share in a note to the consolidated financial statements. Upon adoption, pro forma disclosure will no longer be an alternative. SFAS No. 123R also requires the benefits of tax deductions in excess of recognized compensation cost to be reported as a financing cash flow rather than as an operating cash flow as required under current literature. This requirement will reduce net operating cash flows and increase net financing cash flows in periods after adoption. While we cannot estimate what those amounts will be in the future, the amount of operating cash flows recognized for such deductions were $62.6 million, $25.6 million and $3.2 million in 2004, 2003 and 2002, respectively. We will begin to apply SFAS No. 123R using an appropriate fair value model as of the interim reporting period ending September 30, 2005. Based on stock options outstanding as of December 31, 2004, we estimate approximately $2.1 million in related expense to be recorded during 2005.

QUANTITATIVE AND QUALITATIVE DISCLOSURES ABOUT MARKET RISK

Market risk is the risk of loss arising from adverse changes in market rates and prices, such as interest rates, foreign currency exchange rates and commodity prices. Our primary exposure to market risk is interest rate risk associated with our long-term debt. We attempt to limit our exposure to interest rate risk by managing the mix of our long-term fixed-rate borrowings and short-term borrowings under the Revolving Facility. Borrowings under the Revolving Facility bear interest at a margin above the Alternate Base Rate or the Eurodollar Rate (each as defined in the Revolving Facility) as selected by us. However, the amount of outstanding borrowings is expected to fluctuate and may be reduced from time to time. The Revolving Facility matures in December 2009.

The following table provides information about our long-term debt at December 31, 2004 (see also "Description of Certain Indebtedness and Capital Stock") (amounts in thousands):

	Maturity date	Face amount	Carrying value	Estimated fair value
Revolving Facility at a weighted average interest rate of approximately 4.9%	December 2009	$ 1,000,000	$ 51,500	$ 51,500
6½% senior subordinated notes	February 2014	450,000	450,000	464,625
6% senior notes	April 2012	450,000	448,354	460,125
6⅞% senior subordinated notes	March 2016	350,000	350,000	365,750
9⅞% senior subordinated notes	July 2010	375,000	17,332	18,225
8⅜% senior notes	February 2008	400,000	16,894	17,401
Other debt, interest at 6.0%	2007–2008	6,103	6,060	6,060
Market value of interest rate swaps		(1,927)	(1,927)	(1,927)
Total		$ 3,029,176	$ 1,338,213	$1,381,759

We are also exposed to market risk in the form of fluctuations in interest rates and their potential impact upon our debt. This market risk is managed by utilizing derivative financial instruments in accordance with established policies and procedures. We evaluate our exposure to market risk by monitoring interest rates in the marketplace, and do not utilize derivative financial instruments for trading purposes. Our derivative financial instruments consist exclusively of interest rate swap agreements. Interest differentials resulting from these agreements are recorded on an accrual basis as an adjustment to interest expense. Interest rate swaps related to debt are matched with specific fixed-rate debt obligations.

The following table provides information about our financial instruments that are sensitive to changes in interest rates (amounts in thousands):

| | | | | | | During the year ending December 31, | |
	2005	2006	2007	2008	2009	Thereafter	Total
Long-term debt (including current portion):							
Fixed-rate	$16,894	$ –	$ 5,334	$ –	$ –	$1,265,687	$1,287,915
Average interest rate	8.38%	–	6.00%	–	–	6.50%	6.52%
Variable-rate	$ 23	$ 25	$ 262	$ 415	$ 51,500	$ –	$ 52,225
Average interest rate	6.00%	6.00%	6.00%	6.00%	4.93%	–	4.94%
Interest rate swaps:							
Notional amount	$ –	$ –	$ –	$ –	$ –	$ 250,000	$ 250,000
Average payable rate	–	–	–	–	–	3.75%	3.75%
Average receivable rate	–	–	–	–	–	6.33%	6.33%

CONSOLIDATED BALANCE SHEETS

(amounts in thousands, except share data)

	December 31, 2004	December 31, 2003
ASSETS		
Current assets:		
Cash and cash equivalents	$ 68,417	$ 62,272
Receivables, net	21,452	28,224
Inventories	5,459	5,110
Prepaid gaming tax	16,432	14,940
Prepaid expenses	7,761	7,114
Deferred income tax	–	16,804
TOTAL CURRENT ASSETS	119,521	134,464
Property and equipment, net	1,367,957	1,158,299
Goodwill and other intangibles, net	155,775	148,717
Land held for development	167,729	119,197
Investments in joint ventures	106,598	86,425
Other assets, net	128,004	98,870
Total assets	$ 2,045,584	$ 1,745,972
LIABILITIES AND STOCKHOLDERS' EQUITY		
Current liabilities:		
Current portion of long-term debt	$ 16,917	$ 22
Accounts payable	10,351	20,438
Construction contracts payable	36,298	–
Accrued expenses and other current liabilities	112,450	121,856
TOTAL CURRENT LIABILITIES	176,016	142,316
Long-term debt, less current portion	1,321,296	1,168,935
Deferred income tax, net	20,094	65,285
Other long-term liabilities, net	39,257	29,497
TOTAL LIABILITIES	1,556,663	1,406,033
Commitments and Contingencies		
Stockholders' equity:		
Common stock, par value $0.01; authorized 135,000,000 shares; 77,298,227 and 70,912,227 shares issued	561	497
Treasury stock, 10,185,343 and 10,121,677 shares, at cost	(137,714)	(134,534)
Additional paid-in capital	567,939	387,973
Deferred compensation – restricted stock	(77,598)	(27,003)
Accumulated other comprehensive loss	(611)	(1,334)
Retained earnings	136,344	114,340
TOTAL STOCKHOLDERS' EQUITY	488,921	339,939
Total liabilities and stockholders' equity	$ 2,045,584	$ 1,745,972

The accompanying notes are an integral part of these consolidated financial statements.

CONSOLIDATED STATEMENTS OF OPERATIONS

(amounts in thousands, except per share data)

	For the years ended December 31,		
	2004	2003	2002
Operating revenues:			
Casino	$ 730,584	$ 648,664	$ 638,113
Food and beverage	140,332	133,676	133,811
Room	57,057	50,460	48,579
Other	42,008	45,943	40,790
Management fees	84,618	46,711	4,853
GROSS REVENUES	1,054,599	925,454	866,146
Promotional allowances	(67,857)	(67,365)	(73,281)
NET REVENUES	986,742	858,089	792,865
Operating costs and expenses:			
Casino	273,816	265,203	258,383
Food and beverage	100,548	87,783	78,738
Room	21,053	19,580	19,000
Other	16,820	15,452	16,276
Selling, general and administrative	172,923	161,643	161,038
Corporate expense	47,189	33,039	31,946
Development expense	10,683	4,306	–
Depreciation and amortization	85,807	73,144	72,783
Preopening expenses	848	–	–
Impairment loss	–	18,868	8,791
Litigation settlement	–	38,000	–
	729,687	717,018	646,955
OPERATING INCOME	257,055	141,071	145,910
Earnings from joint ventures	26,524	20,604	11,293
OPERATING INCOME AND EARNINGS FROM JOINT VENTURES	283,579	161,675	157,203
Other income (expense):			
Interest expense	(76,921)	(92,940)	(96,795)
Interest and other expense from joint ventures	(4,485)	(7,233)	(6,272)
Interest income	122	4,873	106
Loss on early retirement of debt	(93,265)	–	(5,808)
Other	(3,801)	1,802	1,322
	(178,350)	(93,498)	(107,447)
INCOME BEFORE INCOME TAXES AND CUMULATIVE EFFECT OF CHANGE IN ACCOUNTING PRINCIPLE	105,229	68,177	49,756
Income tax provision	(38,879)	(23,834)	(18,508)
INCOME BEFORE CUMULATIVE EFFECT OF CHANGE IN ACCOUNTING PRINCIPLE	66,350	44,343	31,248
Cumulative effect of change in accounting principle, net of applicable income tax benefit of $7,170	–	–	(13,316)
Net income	$ 66,350	$ 44,343	$ 17,932
Basic and diluted earnings per common share:			
Income before cumulative effect of change in accounting principle:			
Basic	$ 1.03	$ 0.76	$ 0.54
Diluted	$ 1.00	$ 0.72	$ 0.51
Net income:			
Basic	$ 1.03	$ 0.76	$ 0.31
Diluted	$ 1.00	$ 0.72	$ 0.30
Weighted average common shares outstanding:			
Basic	64,362	58,371	57,845
Diluted	66,264	61,850	60,730
Dividends paid per common share	$ 0.685	$ 0.250	$ –

The accompanying notes are an integral part of these consolidated financial statements.

CONSOLIDATED STATEMENTS OF STOCKHOLDERS' EQUITY

(amounts in thousands)

	Common stock	Treasury stock	Additional paid-in capital	Deferred compensation restricted stock	Accumulated other comprehensive loss	Retained earnings	Total stockholders' equity
Balances, December 31, 2001	$ 441	$ (99,248)	$ 300,254	$ (19,510)	$ –	$ 66,967	$ 248,904
Exercise of stock options	11	–	12,322	–	–	–	12,333
Issuance of restricted stock	2	–	3,693	(3,695)	–	–	–
Amortization of deferred compensation	–	–	–	2,973	–	–	2,973
Purchase of treasury stock, at							
cost (743 shares)	–	(10,214)	–	–	–	–	(10,214)
Green Valley Ranch Station							
interest rate swap market valuation							
adjustment, net of income taxes	–	–	–	–	(1,695)	–	(1,695)
Other	–	–	445	–	–	–	445
Net income	–	–	–	–	–	17,932	17,932
Balances, December 31, 2002	454	(109,462)	316,714	(20,232)	(1,695)	84,899	270,678
Exercise of stock options	39	–	58,724	–	–	–	58,763
Issuance of restricted stock	4	–	11,468	(11,472)	–	–	–
Amortization of deferred compensation	–	–	–	3,201	–	–	3,201
Purchase of treasury stock, at							
cost (1,391 shares)	–	(25,072)	–	–	–	–	(25,072)
Green Valley Ranch Station							
interest rate swap market valuation							
adjustment, net of income taxes	–	–	–	–	361	–	361
Dividends paid	–	–	–	–	–	(14,902)	(14,902)
Other	–	–	1,067	1,500	–	–	2,567
Net income	–	–	–	–	–	44,343	44,343
Balances, December 31, 2003	497	(134,534)	387,973	(27,003)	(1,334)	114,340	339,939
Exercise of stock options	52	–	117,584	–	–	–	117,636
Issuance of restricted stock, net	12	–	61,759	(61,771)	–	–	–
Amortization of deferred compensation	–	–	–	9,676	–	–	9,676
Purchase of treasury stock, at							
cost (64 shares)	–	(3,180)	–	–	–	–	(3,180)
Green Valley Ranch Station							
interest rate swap market valuation							
adjustment, net of income taxes	–	–	–	–	723	–	723
Dividends paid	–	–	–	–	–	(44,346)	(44,346)
Other	–	–	623	1,500	–	–	2,123
Net income	–	–	–	–	–	66,350	66,350
Balances, December 31, 2004	$ 561	$ (137,714)	$ 567,939	$ (77,598)	$ (611)	$ 136,344	$ 488,921

The accompanying notes are an integral part of these consolidated financial statements.

CONSOLIDATED STATEMENTS OF CASH FLOWS

(amounts in thousands)

	For the years ended December 31,		
	2004	2003	2002
Cash flows from operating activities:			
NET INCOME	$ 66,350	$ 44,343	$ 17,932
Adjustments to reconcile net income to net cash provided by operating activities:			
Depreciation and amortization	85,807	73,144	72,783
Tax benefit from exercise of stock options	62,643	25,620	3,194
Impairment loss	–	18,868	8,791
Earnings from joint ventures, net	(22,039)	(13,371)	(5,021)
Amortization of debt discount and issuance costs	2,945	3,156	4,082
Loss on early retirement of debt	93,265	–	5,808
Cumulative effect of change in accounting principle	–	–	20,486
Changes in assets and liabilities:			
Receivables, net	6,772	(8,291)	2,432
Inventories and prepaid expenses	(2,488)	(3,264)	856
Deferred income tax	(28,174)	(449)	12,739
Accounts payable	(10,087)	11,904	(18,156)
Accrued expenses and other current liabilities	(9,619)	41,713	3,992
Other, net	16,221	3,078	2,980
TOTAL ADJUSTMENTS	195,246	152,108	114,966
NET CASH PROVIDED BY OPERATING ACTIVITIES	261,596	196,451	132,898
Cash flows from investing activities:			
Capital expenditures	(305,156)	(179,655)	(20,138)
Note receivable	–	34,487	(24,086)
Purchase of land held for development	(76,879)	(19,117)	(4,925)
Proceeds from sale of land, property and equipment	28,090	6,670	13,123
Investments in joint ventures	–	2,329	(60)
Accrued construction contracts payable	99,158	–	–
Payments on construction contracts	(62,860)	–	(5,534)
Other, net	(19,467)	(29,031)	(18,773)
NET CASH USED IN INVESTING ACTIVITIES	(337,114)	(184,317)	(60,393)
Cash flows from financing activities:			
(Payments) borrowings under bank facility with maturity dates less than three months, net	(75,500)	74,800	(25,900)
Borrowings under bank facility, maturity dates greater than three months	–	310,000	135,000
Payments under bank facility, maturity dates greater than three months	(50,000)	(385,000)	(40,000)
Principal payments on notes payable, net	(22)	(122)	(3,560)
Purchase of treasury stock	(3,180)	(25,072)	(10,214)
Exercise of stock options	54,993	33,143	9,139
Proceeds from interest rate swap termination	–	–	15,303
Redemption of senior subordinated notes	(1,028,815)	–	(155,685)
Proceeds from the issuance of senior notes	1,248,214	–	–
Payment of dividends	(44,346)	(14,902)	–
Debt issuance costs	(19,429)	(792)	(3,665)
Other, net	(252)	(1,256)	299
NET CASH PROVIDED BY (USED IN) FINANCING ACTIVITIES	81,663	(9,201)	(79,283)
Cash and cash equivalents:			
Increase (decrease) in cash and cash equivalents	6,145	2,933	(6,778)
Balance, beginning of year	62,272	59,339	66,117
Balance, end of year	$ 68,417	$ 62,272	$ 59,339
Supplemental cash flow disclosures:			
Cash paid for interest, net of $6,968, $3,496 and $2,065 capitalized	$ 62,832	$ 91,629	$ 92,553
Cash (received) paid for income taxes, net	$ (2,558)	$ 1,329	$ (2,567)
Supplemental disclosure of non-cash items:			
Investment in MPM	$ –	$ 6,082	$ –

The accompanying notes are an integral part of these consolidated financial statements.

Notes to Consolidated Financial Statements

1. Summary of Significant Accounting Policies and Basis of Presentation

Basis of Presentation and Organization

Station Casinos, Inc. (the "Company"), a Nevada corporation, is a gaming and entertainment company that currently owns and operates eight major hotel/casino properties (one of which is 50% owned) and five smaller casino properties (one of which is 50% owned), in the Las Vegas metropolitan area, as well as manages a casino for a Native American tribe. The accompanying consolidated financial statements include the accounts of the Company and its wholly owned subsidiaries, Palace Station, Boulder Station, Texas Station, Sunset Station, Santa Fe Station, Fiesta Rancho, Fiesta Henderson, Wild Wild West, Wildfire, Magic Star and Gold Rush. The Company also consolidates MPM Enterprises, LLC ("MPM"), in which it owns a 50% interest and is required to be consolidated. The Company also owns a 50% interest in Barley's and Green Valley Ranch Station and a 6.7% interest in the Palms Casino Resort, which are accounted for under the equity method. The Company is the managing partner for both Barley's and Green Valley Ranch Station. In addition, the Company manages Thunder Valley Casino ("Thunder Valley") in Sacramento, California on behalf of the United Auburn Indian Community ("UAIC") under a management and development contract, which expires on June 8, 2010. All significant intercompany accounts and transactions have been eliminated.

Acquisitions

On August 2, 2004, the Company acquired Magic Star and Gold Rush casinos in Henderson, Nevada. The Company spent approximately $19.8 million for the acquisitions and enhancements to the facilities. The acquisitions were accounted for using the purchase method of accounting. The purchase price was allocated based on estimated fair values at the date of acquisition. A total of approximately $8.2 million, representing the excess of acquisition cost over the estimated fair value of the tangible net assets was allocated to goodwill.

Use of Estimates

The preparation of financial statements in conformity with accounting principles generally accepted in the United States requires management to make estimates and assumptions for items such as slot club program liability, self-insurance reserves, bad debt reserves, estimated useful lives assigned to fixed assets, asset impairment, purchase price allocations made in connection with acquisitions and the calculation of the income tax liabilities, that affect the reported amounts of assets and liabilities and disclosure of contingent assets and liabilities at the date of the financial statements and the reported amounts of revenues and expenses during the reporting period. Actual results may differ from those estimates.

Cash and Cash Equivalents

Cash and cash equivalents includes cash on hand at our properties, as well as investments purchased with an original maturity of 90 days or less.

Inventories

Inventories are stated at the lower of cost or market; cost being determined on a first-in, first-out basis.

Property and Equipment

Property and equipment are stated at cost. Depreciation and amortization are computed using the straight-line method over the estimated useful lives of the assets or the terms of the capitalized lease, whichever is less. Costs of major improvements are capitalized, while costs of normal repairs and maintenance are charged to expense as incurred.

The Company evaluates its property and equipment and other long-lived assets for impairment in accordance with Statement of Financial Accounting Standards ("SFAS") No. 144, "Accounting for the Impairment or Disposal of Long-Lived Assets." For assets to be disposed of, the Company recognizes the asset to be sold at the lower of carrying value or fair market value less costs of disposal. Fair market value for assets to be disposed of is generally estimated based on comparable asset sales, solicited offers or a discounted cash flow model. For assets to be held and used, the Company reviews fixed assets for impairment whenever indicators of impairment exist. If an indicator of impairment exists, the Company compares the estimated future cash flows of the asset, on an undiscounted basis, to the carrying value of the asset. If the undiscounted cash flows exceed the carrying value, no impairment is indicated. If the undiscounted cash flows do not exceed the carrying value, then an impairment is measured based on fair value compared to carrying value, with fair value typically based on a discounted cash flow model. The consolidated financial statements reflect all adjustments required by SFAS No. 144 as of December 31, 2004.

Capitalization of Interest

The Company capitalizes interest costs associated with debt incurred in connection with major construction projects. Interest capitalization ceases once the project is substantially complete or no longer undergoing construction activities to prepare it for its intended use. When no debt is specifically identified as being incurred in connection with such construction projects, the Company capitalizes interest on amounts expended on the project at the Company's weighted average cost of borrowed money. Interest capitalized was approximately $7.0 million, $3.5 million and $2.1 million for the years ended December 31, 2004, 2003 and 2002, respectively.

Goodwill and Other Intangibles

The Financial Accounting Standards Board ("FASB") issued SFAS No. 142, "Goodwill and Other Intangible Assets", in June 2001. SFAS No. 142 changed the accounting for goodwill from an amortization method to an impairment only approach. Amortization of goodwill, including goodwill recorded in past business combinations, ceased upon the adoption of SFAS No. 142. The Company implemented SFAS No. 142 on January 1, 2002 and tested for impairment in accordance with the provisions of SFAS No. 142 in the first quarter of 2002 and will annually perform such test in the fourth quarter of each subsequent year. As a result of an independent third party appraisal, the Company recorded an impairment loss of $13.3 million, net of the applicable tax benefit, during 2002 related to Fiesta Rancho, which is shown as a cumulative effect of a change in accounting principle in the Company's consolidated statements of operations. Fiesta Rancho was purchased in early 2001, and there were no events or changes in circumstances ("triggering events") during the course of 2001 that would have indicated the recoverability of the carrying amount of the property should be assessed. As a result, there was no requirement to test for impairment under the provisions of SFAS No. 121, which was the primary literature regarding the impairment of an asset prior to the adoption of SFAS No. 142. The Company tested for impairment of goodwill in the fourth quarter of 2002 and determined that there was no impairment. The Company tested for impairment of goodwill in the fourth quarter of 2003 and recorded an impairment loss of $17.5 million at Fiesta Rancho as a result of reduced growth assumptions. The Company tested for impairment of goodwill in the fourth quarter of 2004 and determined there was no impairment.

Also, in connection with the acquisition of Fiesta Rancho, the Company acquired the customer list and is amortizing it over five years. The customer list was valued at $5.0 million at the time of the purchase and as of December 31, 2004, had a net book value of approximately $1.2 million.

Debt Issuance Costs

Debt issuance costs incurred in connection with the issuance of long-term debt are capitalized and amortized to interest expense over the expected terms of the related debt agreements and are included in other assets on the Company's consolidated balance sheets.

Preopening Expenses

Preopening expenses have been expensed as incurred. The construction phase of a project typically covers a period of 12 to 24 months. The majority of preopening costs are incurred in the three months prior to opening. During the year ended December 31, 2004, the Company incurred preopening expenses of $0.8 million related to the development of Red Rock (see Note 10).

Interest Rate Swaps

From time to time, the Company uses interest rate swaps and similar financial instruments to assist in managing interest incurred on its long-term debt. The difference between amounts received and paid under such agreements, as well as any costs or fees, is recorded as a reduction of, or addition to, interest expense as incurred over the life of the swap or similar financial instrument (see Note 9).

Revenues and Promotional Allowances

The Company recognizes as casino revenues the net win from gaming activities, which is the difference between gaming wins and losses. All other revenues are recognized as the service is provided. Revenues include the retail value of food, beverage, rooms, entertainment and merchandise provided on a complimentary basis to customers. Such amounts are then deducted from revenues as promotional allowances on the Company's consolidated statements of operations. The estimated departmental costs of providing such promotional allowances are included in casino costs and expenses and consist of the following (amounts in thousands):

	For the years ended December 31,		
	2004	2003	2002
Food and beverage	$ 59,391	$ 57,985	$ 59,781
Room	3,489	3,119	3,023
Other	2,891	3,057	2,899
Total	$ 65,771	$ 64,161	$ 65,703

The Company's Boarding Pass and Amigo Club player rewards programs (the "Programs") allow customers to redeem points earned from their gaming activity at all Station and Fiesta properties for complimentary food, beverage, rooms, entertainment and merchandise. At the time redeemed, the retail value of complimentaries under the Programs are recorded as revenue with a corresponding offsetting amount included in promotional allowances. The cost associated with complimentary food, beverage, rooms, entertainment and merchandise redeemed under the Programs is recorded in casino costs and expenses. The Company also records a liability for the estimated cost of the outstanding points under the Programs.

Related Party Transactions

The Company has entered into various related party transactions, which consist primarily of lease payments related to ground leases at Boulder Station and Texas Station and the purchase of Wildfire. The expenses related to these related party ground lease transactions were approximately $5.7 million, $5.4 million and $5.1 million for the years ended December 31, 2004, 2003 and 2002, respectively. In addition, on January 27, 2003, the

Company purchased substantially all of the assets of Wildfire for $8.0 million from Bauchman Gaming Ventures, LLC, a company owned by the two brothers-in-law of Scott M Nielson, the Company's Executive Vice President and Chief Development Officer.

Earnings Applicable to Common Stock

In accordance with the provisions of SFAS No. 128, "Earnings Per Share", basic EPS is computed by dividing net income applicable to common stock by the weighted average common shares outstanding during the period. Diluted EPS reflects the additional dilution for all potentially dilutive securities such as stock options.

The weighted average number of common shares used in the calculation of basic and diluted earnings per share consisted of the following (amounts in thousands):

	For the years ended December 31,		
	2004	2003	2002
Weighted average common shares outstanding			
(used in calculation of basic earnings per share)	64,362	58,371	57,845
Potential dilution from the assumed exercise of stock options	1,902	3,479	2,885
Weighted average common and common equivalent shares outstanding			
(used in calculation of diluted earnings per share)	66,264	61,850	60,730

The number of antidilutive stock options as of December 31, 2004, 2003 and 2002 was 0, 28,000 and 0.2 million, respectively.

Stock-Based Employee Compensation

The Company applies APB Opinion No. 25 and related interpretations in accounting for its stock-based employee compensation programs. Accordingly, compensation expense recognized was different than what would have been otherwise recognized under the fair value based method defined in SFAS No. 123, "Accounting for Stock-Based Compensation". Had compensation expense for the plans been determined in accordance with SFAS No. 123, the effect on the Company's net income and basic and diluted earnings per common share would have been as follows (amounts in thousands, except per share data):

	For the years ended December 31,		
	2004	2003	2002
Net income:			
As reported	$ 66,350	$ 44,343	$ 17,932
Stock-based compensation expense reported in net income	404	694	289
Stock-based compensation expense under fair value method	(6,029)	(8,175)	(7,022)
Pro forma net income	$ 60,725	$ 36,862	$ 11,199
Earnings per common share:			
Basic – as reported	$ 1.03	$ 0.76	$ 0.31
Basic – pro forma	0.94	0.63	0.19
Diluted – as reported	$ 1.00	$ 0.72	$ 0.30
Diluted – pro forma	0.92	0.60	0.18

The fair value of each option grant is estimated on the date of grant using the Black-Scholes option-pricing method with the following assumptions:

	For the years ended December 31,		
	2004	2003	2002
Expected dividend yield	–	1.63%	–
Expected stock price volatility	–	54.30%	56.34%
Risk-free interest rate	–	2.97%	3.82%
Expected average life of options (years)	–	3.42	4.42
Weighted average fair value per option granted	–	$ 7.53	$ 6.69

There were no stock option grants during 2004 therefore there is no fair value assumptions. Because the SFAS No. 123 method of accounting has not been applied to options granted prior to April 1, 1995, the resulting pro forma net income may not be representative of that to be expected in future years.

Operating Segments

SFAS No. 131, "Disclosures about Segments of an Enterprise and Related Information", requires separate financial information be disclosed for all operating segments of a business. The Company believes that it meets the "economic similarity" criteria established by SFAS No. 131, and as a result, the Company aggregates all of its properties into one operating segment. All of our properties offer the same products, cater to the same customer base, are all located in the greater Las Vegas, Nevada area, have the same regulatory and tax structure, share the same marketing techniques and are all directed by a centralized management structure.

Recently Issued Accounting Standards

In December 2004, the FASB issued Statement of Financial Accounting Standards No. 123R (Revised 2004), "Share-Based Payment" ("SFAS No. 123R"), which requires that the compensation cost relating to share-based payment transactions be recognized in financial statements based on alternative fair value models. The share-based compensation cost will be measured based on fair value models of the equity or liability instruments issued. The Company currently discloses pro forma compensation expense quarterly and annually by calculating the stock option grants' fair value using the Black-Scholes model and disclosing the impact on net income and net income per share in a note to the consolidated financial statements. Upon adoption, pro forma disclosure will no longer be an alternative. The table above reflects the estimated impact that such a change in accounting treatment would have had on our net income and net income per share if it had been in effect during the years ended December 31, 2004, 2003 and 2002. SFAS No. 123R also requires the benefits of tax deductions in excess of recognized compensation cost to be reported as a financing cash flow rather than as an operating cash flow as required under current literature. This requirement will reduce net operating cash flows and increase net financing cash flows in periods after adoption. While the Company cannot estimate what those amounts will be in the future, the amount of operating cash flows recognized for such deductions were $62.6 million, $25.6 million and $3.2 million in 2004, 2003 and 2002, respectively. The Company will begin to apply SFAS No. 123R using an appropriate fair value model as of the interim reporting period ending September 30, 2005. Based on stock options outstanding as of December 31, 2004, the Company estimates approximately $2.1 million in expense to be recorded during 2005.

Reclassifications

Certain amounts in the December 31, 2003 and 2002 consolidated financial statements have been reclassified to conform to the December 31, 2004 presentation. These reclassifications had no effect on the previously reported net income.

2. RECEIVABLES

Components of receivables are as follows (amounts in thousands):

	December 31,	
	2004	2003
Casino	$ 5,554	$ 7,166
Hotel	3,723	2,428
Management fees	8,168	6,301
Income tax	172	7,181
Other	5,837	8,034
	23,454	31,110
Allowance for doubtful accounts	(2,002)	(2,886)
Receivables, net	$ 21,452	$ 28,224

3. PROPERTY AND EQUIPMENT

Property and equipment consists of the following (amounts in thousands):

		December 31,	
	Estimated life (years)	2004	2003
Land	–	$ 154,724	$ 140,043
Buildings and improvements	10 – 45	946,243	901,347
Furniture, fixtures and equipment	3 – 7	472,599	392,818
Construction in progress	–	241,485	99,455
		1,815,051	1,533,663
Accumulated depreciation and amortization		(447,094)	(375,364)
Property and equipment, net		$1,367,957	$1,158,299

At December 31, 2004 and 2003, substantially all property and equipment of the Company is pledged as collateral for long-term debt.

4. Land Held for Development

As of December 31, 2004, the Company had $167.7 million of land held for development that consists primarily of five sites that are owned or leased, which comprise 198 acres in the Las Vegas valley and 188 acres in the Sacramento area near Thunder Valley. The Durango site, located at the intersection of Durango Road and the Southern Beltway/Interstate 215 in the southwest quadrant of Las Vegas, currently consists of 67 acres. The Company also owns a 49-acre gaming-entitled parcel in southwest Las Vegas at the intersection of Flamingo Road and Interstate 215. During the year ended December 31, 2004, the Company purchased approximately 54 acres of land in a gaming enterprise district on the southern end of Las Vegas Boulevard at Cactus Avenue for approximately $33.9 million. In addition, the Company leases and has an option to purchase 2.5 acres adjacent to this site. On October 1, 2004, the Company purchased approximately 26 acres of real property and improvements formerly known as the Castaways Hotel Casino and Bowling Center (the "Castaways") in Las Vegas, Nevada, for $33.75 million. The Castaways closed on January 26, 2004, shortly after its former owners filed for bankruptcy. The Company is currently evaluating the potential uses of the property, but does not believe it is competitive and does not intend to operate the facility in its current state.

In April 2004, the Company sold a 27-acre parcel of land, after removing the gaming entitlements, located at the intersection of Boulder Highway and Nellis Boulevard for net proceeds of approximately $10.5 million. In July 2004, the Company sold a 68-acre parcel of land, after removing the gaming entitlements, located at the intersection of Boulder Highway and Tropicana Avenue in eastern Las Vegas for net proceeds of approximately $15.2 million. As a result of the sale of these parcels of land, the Company recorded a loss of approximately $2.7 million for the year ended December 31, 2004.

The Company also has acquired or is under contract to acquire approximately 58 acres of land on which Wild Wild West is located and the surrounding area of which, approximately 27 acres have been acquired as of December 31, 2004. The Company has exercised its option to purchase the 19-acre parcel of leased land on which Wild Wild West is located. Pursuant to the lease, the purchase will occur in July 2005 at a purchase price of approximately $36 million. No amounts related to this purchase option have been recorded on the Company's consolidated balance sheets. The Company has also agreed to purchase an additional 12 acres of land and is expected to close on these transactions in the first quarter of 2005.

The Company has acquired certain parcels of land in the Las Vegas valley and near Sacramento, California as part of its future development activities. The Company's decision whether to proceed with any new gaming or development opportunity is dependent upon future economic and regulatory factors, the availability of financing and competitive and strategic considerations. As many of these considerations are beyond the Company's control, no assurances can be made that it will be able to secure additional, acceptable financing in order to proceed with any particular project.

5. Investments in Joint Ventures

The Company has investments in two 50% owned joint ventures, Green Valley Ranch Station and Barley's, and a 6.7% investment in a joint venture that owns the Palms Casino Resort in Las Vegas, Nevada, that are accounted for under the equity method. Under the equity method, original investments are recorded at cost and adjusted by the Company's share of earnings, losses and distributions of the joint ventures. The investment balance also includes interest capitalized during the construction period, which is amortized against the earnings of the joint venture. Investments in joint ventures consist of the following (amounts in thousands):

	December 31,	
	2004	2003
Green Valley Ranch Station (50.0%)	$ 85,274	$ 66,484
Barley's (50.0%)	2,984	2,899
Palms Casino Resort (6.7%)	18,340	17,042
Investments in joint ventures	$ 106,598	$ 86,425

Summarized balance sheet information for the joint ventures is as follows (amounts in thousands):

	December 31,	
	2004	2003
Current assets	$ 72,451	$ 51,551
Property and equipment and other assets, net	633,592	525,515
Current liabilities	60,605	37,977
Long-term debt and other liabilities	243,430	196,399
Stockholders' equity	402,008	342,690

Summarized results of operations for the joint ventures are as follows (amounts in thousands):

	For the years ended December 31,		
	2004	2003	2002
Net revenues	$ 385,838	$ 327,190	$ 276,051
Operating costs and expenses	302,135	263,481	236,817
OPERATING INCOME	83,703	63,709	39,234
Interest and other expense, net	10,069	12,734	19,450
Net income	$ 73,634	$ 50,975	$ 19,784

The operating earnings from these joint ventures are shown as a separate line item on the Company's consolidated statements of operations after operating income. In addition, interest and other expense from these joint ventures is shown as a separate component under other income (expense) in the Company's consolidated statements of operations. The following table identifies the total equity earnings from joint ventures (amounts in thousands):

	For the years ended December 31,		
	2004	2003	2002
Operating earnings from joint ventures	$ 26,524	$ 20,604	$ 11,293
Interest and other expense from joint ventures	(4,485)	(7,233)	(6,272)
Net earnings from joint ventures	$ 22,039	$ 13,371	$ 5,021

Green Valley Ranch Station

Green Valley Ranch Station is owned by a 50/50 joint venture between the Company and GCR Gaming. In December 2004, Green Valley Ranch Station entered into a new $250 million Second Amended and Restated Loan Agreement (the "Green Valley Facility"), which refinanced the existing $250 million revolving credit facility and term loan. The Green Valley Facility extends the maturity of the revolving portion to December 2009 and the term loan portion to December 2011. The outstanding balance of the Green Valley Ranch Station revolving credit facility as of December 31, 2004, was approximately $200 million.

6. MANAGEMENT FEES

The Company manages Thunder Valley for the UAIC and receives a management fee equal to 24% of net income (as defined in the management agreement). The Company is also the managing partner for both Green Valley Ranch Station and Barley's and receives a management fee equal to 2% of revenues and approximately 5% of Earnings Before Interest, Taxes, Depreciation and Amortization ("EBITDA") from Green Valley Ranch Station and 10% of EBITDA from Barley's. The Company's management fees are included in net revenues on the Company's consolidated statements of operations.

United Auburn Indian Community

The Company has entered into a Development Services Agreement and a Management Agreement with the UAIC. The Company's seven-year Management Agreement was approved by the National Indian Gaming Commission ("NIGC") and expires in June 2010. Pursuant to those agreements, and in compliance with a Memorandum of Understanding entered into by the UAIC and Placer County, California, the Company and the UAIC developed Thunder Valley, a gaming and entertainment facility on approximately 49 acres located approximately seven miles north of Interstate 80, in Placer County, California, near Sacramento, which opened on June 9, 2003. In June 2004, the UAIC successfully negotiated a new Tribal-State Gaming Compact ("Amended Compact") with the State of California, which has been approved by the United States Department of the Interior (the "DOI"). The Amended Compact allows an unlimited number of slot machines at Thunder Valley and extends the term an additional 10 years to 2030. The Amended Compact also includes a revenue sharing agreement with the State of California. The UAIC will pay approximately $33.8 million annually to the State of California commencing in January 2005 and additional fees ranging from $11,000 to $13,200 per machine for any slot machines added above the 1,906 machines that were in operation at Thunder Valley prior to the Amended Compact.

On September 17, 2002, the DOI accepted the land into trust on behalf of the UAIC. The acceptance of the land into trust followed the decision of the United States District Court for the District of Washington, D.C., dismissing a lawsuit filed by the cities of Roseville and Rocklin, California, and Citizens for Safer Communities, which challenged the DOI's decision to accept the land into trust. Immediately following the District Court's decision, the plaintiffs appealed the decision to the United States Court of Appeals for the District of Columbia. On November 14, 2003, the Court of Appeals affirmed the dismissal of the lawsuit by the District Court. On February 15, 2004, Citizens for Safer Communities filed a petition for writ of certiorari with the United States Supreme Court, seeking to appeal the decision of the Court of Appeals. The remaining plaintiffs did not seek to appeal the decision. On April 5, 2004, the United States Supreme Court denied Citizens for Safer Communities' petition for writ of certiorari.

7. ASSET IMPAIRMENT

The Company recorded an impairment loss of approximately $18.9 million and $8.8 million in the years ended December 31, 2003 and 2002, respectively, to adjust the carrying value of its goodwill and other assets to their estimated fair value. The $18.9 million impairment loss in 2003 related to the write-off of approximately $17.5 million in goodwill at Fiesta Rancho in accordance with SFAS No. 142 as a result of reduced growth assumptions. The remaining $1.4 million impairment loss in 2003 was primarily related to the write off of the Company's investment in a new slot product development. The impairment of this asset was based upon a decision by the Company to no longer pursue the development of certain slot products. As a result, all of the development costs that the Company had incurred were written off, as they were deemed to have no value.

During the year ended December 31, 2002, approximately $3.9 million of the impairment loss related to the write-down of certain assets related to the Company's investments in an Internet, intra-state gaming platform and related technology. In May 2002, the Nevada Gaming Commission communicated that it had general concerns regarding the security and reliability of Internet gaming platforms. The impairment of these assets was based upon a decision by the Company to no longer pursue Nevada-based Internet gaming activities as a result of the uncertainty of regulatory approval of these types of activities. As a result, all of the hardware, software and internal development costs that the Company had incurred were written off in 2002, as they were deemed to have no value. In addition, approximately $4.9 million of the impairment loss was related to the Company's option to invest in an Internet wagering business. In February 2002, the Company announced that it intended to purchase a 50% interest in Kerzner Interactive Limited (formerly SunOnline Limited) ("Kerzner Interactive"), a wholly owned subsidiary of Kerzner International Limited (formerly Sun International Hotels Limited) ("Kerzner"). Kerzner Interactive was to be the exclusive vehicle for both Kerzner and the Company to pursue the Internet wagering business. In July 2002, the Company converted its agreement to acquire a 50% interest in Kerzner Interactive into an option to do so, and paid $4.5 million for such option. Kerzner decided to discontinue Kerzner Interactive, as it targeted Internet wagering only from jurisdictions that permitted online gaming. As these jurisdictions became more restrictive in their acceptance of Internet gaming, the market size was reduced and competition intensified, resulting in a substantial decrease in the probability of achieving profitability in the short-to-medium term. As a result, the Company wrote off the option payment and other costs related to this investment in 2002.

8. Accrued Expenses and Other Current Liabilities

Accrued expenses and other current liabilities consist of the following (amounts in thousands):

	December 31,	
	2004	2003
Accrued payroll and related	$ 40,874	$ 24,774
Accrued interest payable	27,524	14,655
Accrued progressives	5,096	4,459
Accrued group insurance	4,194	2,921
Litigation settlement	–	38,000
Other accrued expenses and current liabilities	34,762	37,047
Total accrued expenses and other current liabilities	$ 112,450	$ 121,856

9. Long-term Debt

Long-term debt consists of the following (amounts in thousands):

	December 31,	
	2004	2003
Revolving credit facility, $1.0 billion limit at December 31, 2004, due December 31, 2009, interest at a margin above the Alternate Base Rate or the Eurodollar Rate (4.9% at December 31, 2004)	$ 51,500	$ 177,000
6½% senior subordinated notes, interest payable semi-annually, principal due February 1, 2014, callable February 1, 2009	450,000	–
6% senior notes, interest payable semi-annually, principal due April 1, 2012, callable April 1, 2008, net of unamortized discount of $1.6 million at December 31, 2004	448,354	–
6⅞% senior subordinated notes, interest payable semi-annually, principal due March 1, 2016, callable March 1, 2009	350,000	–
9⅞% senior subordinated notes, interest payable semi-annually, principal due July 1, 2010, callable July 1, 2005, net of unamortized discount of $46 and $1.1 million at December 31, 2004 and 2003, respectively	17,332	373,886
8⅜% senior notes, interest payable semi-annually, principal due February 15, 2008, called February 15, 2005	16,894	400,000
8⅞% senior subordinated notes, interest payable semi-annually, principal due December 1, 2008	–	199,900
Other long-term debt, interest at 6.0% at December 31, 2004, maturity dates ranging from 2007 to 2008	6,060	6,082
TOTAL LONG-TERM DEBT	1,340,140	1,156,868
Current portion of long-term debt	(16,917)	(22)
Market value of interest rate swaps	(1,927)	12,089
Total long-term debt, net	$ 1,321,296	$ 1,168,935

Revolving Facility

In December 2004, the Company increased its availability under its revolving credit facility (the "Revolving Facility") to $1.0 billion and extended the maturity by two years to December 2009. The Revolving Facility contains no principal amortization. The Borrowers are the major operating subsidiaries and the Revolving Facility is secured by substantially all of the Company's assets. Borrowings under the Revolving Facility bear interest at a margin above the Alternate Base Rate or the Eurodollar Rate (each as defined in the Revolving Facility), as selected by the Company. The margin above such rates, and the fee on the unfunded portions of the Revolving Facility, will vary quarterly based on the Company's combined consolidated ratio of debt to Adjusted EBITDA (as defined in the Revolving Facility). As of December 31, 2004, the Borrowers' margin above the Eurodollar Rate on borrowings under the Revolving Facility was 1.38%. The maximum margin for Eurodollar Rate borrowings is 2.13%. The maximum margin for Alternate Base Rate borrowings is 0.88%. As of December 31, 2004, the fee for the unfunded portion of the Revolving Facility was 0.25%.

The Revolving Facility contains certain financial and other covenants. These include a maximum funded debt to Adjusted EBITDA ratio for the Borrowers combined of 2.50 to 1.00 for each quarter and a minimum fixed charge coverage ratio for the preceding four quarters for the Borrowers combined of 1.50 to 1.00 for each quarter. As of December 31, 2004, the Borrowers' funded debt to Adjusted EBITDA ratio was 0.21 to 1.00 and the fixed charge coverage ratio was 2.31 to 1.00. In addition, the Revolving Facility has financial and other covenants, which require that the maximum consolidated funded debt to Adjusted EBITDA ratio can be no more than 5.50 to 1.00 through December 31, 2005, which reduces to 5.25 to 1.00 on March 31, 2006 through December 31, 2006, to 5.00 to 1.00 on March 31, 2007 through December 31, 2007, to 4.75 to 1.00 on March 31, 2008 through December 31, 2008 and to 4.50 to 1.00 on March 31, 2009. Other covenants limit prepayments of indebtedness or rent (including subordinated debt other than re-financings meeting certain criteria), limitations on asset dispositions, limitations on dividends, limitations on indebtedness, limitations on investments and limitations on capital expenditures. As of December 31, 2004, the Company's consolidated funded debt to Adjusted EBITDA ratio was 3.58 to 1.00. The Company has pledged the stock of all of its major subsidiaries.

Senior and Senior Subordinated Notes

During the first quarter of 2004, the Company refinanced substantially all of its senior and senior subordinated notes. The Company issued $1.25 billion in new senior and senior subordinated notes which consists of $450.0 million 6% senior notes due in April 2012, $450.0 million 6$^{1/2}$% senior subordinated notes due in February 2014 and $350.0 million 6 $^{7/8}$% senior subordinated notes due in March 2016. The proceeds from these offerings were used to redeem or repurchase the $199.9 million 8$^{7/8}$% senior subordinated notes due in December 2008, to repurchase $357.6 million of the 9$^{7/8}$% senior subordinated notes due in July 2010, to repurchase $383.1 million of the 8$^{3/8}$% senior notes due in February 2008 and to reduce amounts outstanding under the Revolving Facility. As a result of these redemptions, the Company recorded a loss on early retirement of debt of approximately $93.3 million in the year ended December 31, 2004 to reflect the write-off of the unamortized loan costs, unamortized discount, call premium, tender fee and consent payments which were partially offset by the fair value of the interest rate swaps that were tied directly to the redeemed senior and senior subordinated notes.

On February 15, 2005, the Company redeemed the remaining $16.9 million of outstanding 8$^{3/8}$% senior notes due 2008. As a result of the redemption, the Company will record a loss on early retirement of debt of approximately $0.7 million in the first quarter of 2005 to reflect the write-off of the unamortized loan costs and call premium.

The indentures (the "Indentures") governing the Company's senior subordinated notes (the "Notes") contain certain customary financial and other covenants, which limit the Company and its subsidiaries' ability to incur additional debt. At December 31, 2004, the Company's Consolidated Coverage Ratio (as defined in the Indentures) was 4.07 to 1.00. The Indentures provide that the Company may not incur additional indebtedness, other than specified types of indebtedness, unless the Consolidated Coverage Ratio is at least 2.00 to 1.00. In the event the Company's Consolidated Coverage Ratio is below 2.00 to 1.00, the covenant limits the Company's ability to incur additional indebtedness for borrowings under the Revolving Facility not to exceed the greater of $200 million or 1.5 times Operating Cash Flow (as defined) for the four most recent quarters, plus $15 million. The Indentures also give the holders of the Notes the right to require the Company to purchase the Notes at 101% of the principal amount of the Notes plus accrued interest thereon upon a Change of Control and Rating Decline (each as defined in the Indentures) of the Company. In addition, the indenture governing the Senior Notes contains a limitation on liens the Company can incur.

The Company has entered into various interest rate swaps with members of its bank group to manage interest expense. As of December 31, 2004, the Company has interest rate swaps with a combined notional amount of $250.0 million that are tied directly to the Company's $6\frac{1}{2}$% senior subordinated notes and the Company's 6% senior notes. The interest rate swaps convert a portion of the Company's fixed-rate debt to a floating-rate based upon three and six-month LIBOR rates. At December 31, 2004, the Company pays a weighted average rate based on LIBOR, which approximates 3.75% and receives a weighted average rate of 6.33%. The interest rate swaps terminate in April 2012 and February 2014. The net effect of the interest rate swaps resulted in a reduction in interest expense of $7.3 million, $3.6 million and $10.7 million for the years ended December 31, 2004, 2003 and 2002, respectively.

The interest rate swaps that the Company entered into qualify for the "shortcut" method allowed under SFAS No. 133, "Accounting for Derivative Instruments and Hedging Activities" (and as amended by SFAS No. 138), which allows for an assumption of no ineffectiveness. As such, there is no income statement impact from changes in the fair value of the hedging instruments. Instead, the fair value of the instrument is recorded as an asset or liability on the Company's balance sheet with an offsetting adjustment to the carrying value of the related debt. In accordance with SFAS No. 133, the Company recorded a liability of $2.2 million and an asset of $3.9 million as of December 31, 2004 and 2003, respectively, representing the fair value of the interest rate swaps and a corresponding decrease and increase in long-term debt, as these interest rate swaps are considered highly effective under the criteria established by SFAS No. 133.

In March 2004, the Company terminated an interest rate swap with a notional amount of $50.0 million, which was due to terminate in 2008. The interest rate swap was terminated at its market value and, as a result, the Company received approximately $3.6 million, which is included in the calculation of the net loss on the early retirement of debt as the interest rate swap was tied directly to the redemption of the $400.0 million $8\frac{3}{8}$% senior notes.

In December 2002, the Company terminated an interest rate swap with a notional amount of $100 million, which was due to terminate in 2010. The interest rate swap was terminated at its market value and, as a result, the Company received approximately $9.5 million. This interest rate swap was tied directly to the $375 million $9\frac{7}{8}$% senior subordinated notes. Approximately $357.6 million of the $9\frac{7}{8}$% senior subordinated notes were redeemed in the first quarter of 2004 and, as a result, approximately $7.6 million of the remaining value of this fair value hedge termination was included in the calculation of the net loss on the early retirement of debt.

On October 18, 2002, the Company redeemed its $150 million 9³/₄% senior subordinated notes. The redemption was funded with proceeds from the Revolving Facility. The Company recorded a charge of approximately $10.1 million during the year ended December 31, 2002, to reflect the write-off of the unamortized debt discount, unamortized loan costs and the premium to redeem the $150 million 9³/₄% senior subordinated notes. This charge was partially offset by approximately $5.7 million from the adjusted basis of the debt as a result of the fair value hedge termination that was tied directly to the $150 million 9³/₄% senior subordinated notes, as discussed below. In addition, the Company recorded a loss on early retirement of debt of approximately $1.4 million in 2002 to reflect the write-off of the unamortized loan costs on the previous revolving facility.

In September 2002, the Company terminated an interest rate swap with a notional amount of $150 million, which was due to terminate in 2007. The interest rate swap was terminated at its market value and, as a result, the Company received approximately $5.8 million. This interest rate swap was tied directly to the $150 million 9³/₄% senior subordinated notes. The mark-to-market adjustment was amortized as a reduction of interest expense over the original contract life of the interest rate swap. When the $150 million 9³/₄% senior subordinated notes were redeemed on October 18, 2002, the adjusted basis of the debt as a result of the fair value hedge termination of approximately $5.7 million was included in the calculation of the net loss on the early retirement of the related debt.

The estimated fair value of the Company's long-term debt at December 31, 2004 was approximately $1.38 billion, compared to its book value of approximately $1.34 billion. The estimated fair value amounts were based on quoted market prices on or about December 31, 2004, for the Company's debt securities that are publicly traded. For the Revolving Facility, the fair value approximates the carrying amount of the debt due to the short-term maturities of the individual components of the debt.

Scheduled maturities of long-term debt are as follows (amounts in thousands):

Years ending December 31,

2005	$ 16,917
2006	25
2007	5,596
2008	415
2009	51,500
Thereafter	1,265,687
Total	$ 1,340,140

10. COMMITMENTS AND CONTINGENCIES

Red Rock

In April 2004, we commenced construction of Red Rock Resort Spa and Casino ("Red Rock") located on Charleston Boulevard at the Interstate 215/Charleston interchange in the Summerlin master-planned community in Las Vegas, Nevada. The initial phase of the property is expected to be completed near the end of the first quarter of 2006. We have also announced plans to accelerate the construction of a phase II expansion. Construction on phase II of Red Rock is expected to begin in the latter part of 2005 and is expected to be completed by the end of 2006. The total project will now include over 2,800 slot machines, over 850 hotel rooms, 94,000 square feet of meeting and convention space, a 35,000 square-foot spa, nine full service restaurants, a 16-screen movie theater complex, a night club and private pool club to be operated by Midnight Oil Company, both indoor and outdoor entertainment venues and parking for almost 5,500 vehicles. As a result of an increase in amenities, an upgrade in the quality of finishes throughout the project, general increases in construction cost and addition of the phase II expansion, the total cost of Red Rock is expected to be approximately $800 million, of which approximately $151.3 million has been spent as of December 31, 2004.

Santa Fe Station Expansion

In 2003, the Company began a $52 million expansion at Santa Fe Station. The expansion includes additional casino space, slot machines, a new movie theater complex, an upgrade of the property's bowling center, a new entertainment venue and bar, a new Kid's Quest facility and other amenities as well as removal of the ice arena. The additional slots, upgrade of the bowling center and new entertainment venue were completed in December 2004. The Company believes the remaining items will be completed in the first quarter of 2005 with the exception of the movie theater complex, which will be completed in April 2005. Approximately $35.8 million has been spent on the expansion as of December 31, 2004.

Sunset Station Expansion

The Company is currently expanding Sunset Station to add a bowling center. The cost of the expansion is expected to be approximately $27 million, of which approximately $9.5 million has been spent as of December 31, 2004. The Company believes that the expansion will be completed in April 2005.

Boulder Station Lease

The Company entered into a ground lease for 27 acres of land on which Boulder Station is located. The Company leases this land from KB Enterprises, a company owned by Frank J. Fertitta, Jr. and Victoria K. Fertitta (the "Related Lessor"), the parents of Frank J. Fertitta III, Chairman of the Board and Chief Executive Officer of the Company and Lorenzo J. Fertitta, Vice Chairman and President of the Company. The lease has a maximum term of 65 years, ending in June 2058. The lease provides for monthly payments of $183,333 through June 2008. In July 2008, and every ten years thereafter, the rent will be adjusted by a cost of living factor. In July 2013, and every ten years thereafter, the rent will be adjusted to the product of the fair market value of the land and the greater of (i) the then prevailing annual rate of return for comparably situated property or (ii) 8% per year. In no event will the rent for any period be less than the immediately preceding period. Pursuant to the ground lease, the Company has an option, exercisable at five-year intervals with the next option in June 2008, to purchase the land at fair market value. The Company's leasehold interest in the property is subject to a lien to secure borrowings under the Revolving Facility.

Texas Station Lease

The Company entered into a ground lease for 47 acres of land on which Texas Station is located. The Company leases this land from Texas Gambling Hall & Hotel, Inc., a company owned by the Related Lessor. The lease has a maximum term of 65 years, ending in July 2060. The lease provides for monthly rental payments of $287,500 through June 2005. In July 2005, and every ten years thereafter, the rent will be adjusted by a cost of living factor. In July 2010, and every ten years thereafter, the rent will be adjusted to the product of the fair market value of the land and the greater of (i) the then prevailing annual rate of return being realized for owners of comparable land in Clark County or (ii) 8% per year. In no event will the rent for any period be less than the immediately preceding period. Pursuant to the ground lease, the Company has an option, exercisable at five-year intervals with the next option in May 2005, to purchase the land at fair market value. The Company's leasehold interest in the property is subject to a lien to secure borrowings under the Revolving Facility.

Wild Wild West Lease

The Company exercised its option to purchase the 19-acre parcel of land on which Wild Wild West is located in 2003. Pursuant to the lease, the purchase will take place in July 2005 for approximately $36 million. No amounts related to this purchase option have been recorded on the Company's consolidated balance sheets at December 31, 2004 and 2003. The Company currently leases this land for approximately $2.9 million per year.

Operating Leases

The Company leases several parcels of land, buildings and equipment used in its operations. Leases on various parcels ranging from 2.5 acres to 47 acres have terms expiring between June 2005 and August 2103. Future minimum lease payments required under these operating leases and other noncancelable operating leases are as follows (amounts in thousands):

Years ending December 31,	
2005	$ 11,199
2006	9,058
2007	8,948
2008	8,855
2009	8,841
Thereafter	449,719
Total	$ 496,620

Rent expense totaled approximately $14.9 million, $13.6 million and $12.7 million for the years ended December 31, 2004, 2003 and 2002, respectively.

Green Valley Ranch Station

In the fourth quarter of 2003, the Company began a $125 million expansion at Green Valley Ranch Station. The expansion includes hotel rooms, additional meeting space and an expanded spa facility. Construction of the hotel rooms and additional meeting space was completed in December 2004. Construction of the spa facility is expected to be completed in the first quarter of 2005. In connection with the expansion, Green Valley Ranch Station purchased the lease from the spa operator during 2004. Green Valley Ranch Station also terminated the lease of a restaurant at the property and paid the tenant an agreed upon sum during 2004. As a result, the Company has recorded a reduction in earnings from joint ventures of approximately $3.6 million as of December 31, 2004, which represents its 50% share of the total loss. In accordance with the terms of the current loan, a completion guaranty is required to complete the expansion. The completion guaranty is a joint obligation of both partners.

The Federated Indians of Graton Rancheria

The Company has entered into Development and Management Agreements with the Federated Indians of the Graton Rancheria (the "FIGR"), a federally recognized Native American tribe. Pursuant to those agreements, the Company will assist the FIGR in developing and operating a gaming and entertainment project to be located in Sonoma County, California. The FIGR selected the Company to assist it in designing, developing and financing the project and, upon opening, the Company will manage the facility on behalf of the FIGR. The Management Agreement has a term of seven years from the opening of the facility and the Company will receive a management fee equal to 22% of the facility's net income. The Company will also receive a development fee equal to 2% of the cost of the project upon the opening of the facility.

In August 2003, the Company entered into an option to purchase 360 acres of land just west of the Rohnert Park city limits in Sonoma County, California. The proposed site of the project is bordered by Stony Point Road, Wilfred Avenue and Rohnert Park Expressway, approximately one-half mile from Highway 101 and approximately 43 miles from downtown San Francisco. In October 2003, the FIGR entered into a Memorandum of Understanding with the City of Rohnert Park. Development of the gaming and entertainment project is subject to certain governmental and regulatory approvals, including, but not limited to, negotiating a gaming compact with the State of California, the United State Department of the Interior ("DOI") accepting the land into trust on behalf of the FIGR and approval of the Management Agreement by the National Indian Gaming Commission ("NIGC"). Prior to obtaining third-party financing, the Company will contribute significant financial support to the project. As of December 31, 2004, the Company had advanced approximately $22.4 million toward the development of this project, primarily to perform due diligence and secure real estate for the FIGR project, which is included in other assets, net on the Company's consolidated balance sheets. Funds advanced by the Company are expected to be repaid with the proceeds of the project financing or from the FIGR's gaming revenues. In addition, the Company has agreed to pay approximately $11.3 million of payments upon achieving certain milestones, which will not be reimbursed. As of December 31, 2004, approximately $2.0 million of these payments had been made and were expensed in development expense as incurred. The timing of this type of project is difficult to predict and is dependent upon the receipt of the necessary governmental and regulatory approvals. There can be no assurances when or if these approvals will be obtained.

Gun Lake Tribe

On November 13, 2003, the Company agreed to purchase a 50% interest in MPM Enterprises, LLC, a Michigan limited liability company ("MPM"). Concurrently with the Company's agreement to purchase that interest, MPM and the Match-E-Be-Nash-She-Wish Band of Pottawatomi Indians, a federally recognized Native American tribe commonly referred to as the Gun Lake Tribe ("Gun Lake"), entered into amended Development and Management Agreements, pursuant to which MPM will assist Gun Lake in developing and operating a gaming and entertainment project to be located in Allegan County, Michigan. The Company has agreed to pay $6.0 million for its 50% interest in MPM, which is payable upon achieving certain milestones and is not reimbursable. As of December 31, 2004, approximately $2.0 million of these payments had been made and were expensed in development expense as incurred. An additional $12.0 million in total may be paid by the Company in years six and seven of the amended Management Agreement, subject to certain contingencies. Under the terms of the amended Development Agreement, the Company has agreed to arrange financing for the ongoing development costs and construction of the project. As of December 31, 2004, the Company had advanced approximately $20.2 million toward the development of this project, primarily to secure real estate for the project, which is included in other assets, net on the Company's consolidated balance sheets. Funds advanced by the Company are expected to be repaid from the proceeds of the project financing or from Gun Lake's gaming revenues. The amended Management Agreement has a term of seven years from the opening of the facility and provides for a management fee of 30% of the project's net income to be paid to MPM. Pursuant to the terms of the MPM Operating Agreement, the Company's portion of the management fee is 50% of the first $24 million of management fees earned, 83% of the next $24 million of management fees and 93% of any management fees in excess of $48 million.

The proposed project will be located on approximately 145 acres on Highway 131 near 129th Avenue, approximately 25 miles north of Kalamazoo, Michigan. As currently contemplated, the project will include up to 2,500 slot machines, 75 table games, a buffet and specialty restaurants. Construction of the project includes the conversion of an existing 192,000 square-foot building into the casino and entertainment facility. Development of the gaming and entertainment project and operation of Class III gaming is subject to certain governmental and regulatory approvals, including, but not limited to, the signing of a gaming compact by the Governor of the State of Michigan, the DOI accepting the land into trust on behalf of Gun Lake and approval of the Management Agreement by the NIGC. On February 27, 2004, the DOI issued a Finding Of No Significant Impact with respect to the proposed project. Prior to obtaining third-party financing, the Company will contribute significant financial support to the project. The timing of this type of project is difficult to predict and is dependent upon the receipt of the necessary gonernmental and regulatory approvals. There can be no assurances when or if these approvals will be obtained.

Mechoopda Indian Tribe

The Company has entered into Development and Management Agreements with the Mechoopda Indian Tribe of Chico Rancheria, California (the "MITCR"), a federally recognized Native American tribe. Pursuant to those agreements, the Company will assist the MITCR in developing and operating a gaming and entertainment facility to be located on approximately 650 acres in Butte County, California, at the intersection of State Route 149 and Highway 99, approximately 10 miles southeast of Chico, California and 80 miles north of Sacramento, California. Under the terms of the Development Agreement, the Company has agreed to arrange the financing for the ongoing development costs and construction of the facility. Funds advanced by the Company are expected to be repaid from the proceeds of the facility financing or from the MITCR's gaming revenues. As of December 31, 2004, the Company had advanced approximately $5.8 million toward the development of this project, primarily to secure real estate for future development, which is included in other assets, net on the Company's consolidated balance sheets. In addition, the Company has agreed to pay approximately $2.2 million of payments upon achieving certain milestones, which will not be reimbursed. As of December 31, 2004, $50,000 of these payments had been made and were expensed in development expense as incurred. The Management Agreement has a term of seven years from the opening of the facility and provides for a management fee of 24% of the facility's net income. As currently contemplated, the facility will include approximately 700 slot machines, 12 table games and dining and entertainment amenities. Development of the facility is subject to certain governmental and regulatory approvals, including, but not limited to, negotiating a gaming compact with the State of California, the DOI accepting land into trust on behalf of the MITCR and approval of the Management Agreement by the NIGC. Prior to obtaining third-party financing, the Company will contribute significant financial support to the project. The timing of this type of project is difficult to predict and is dependent upon the receipt of the necessary gonernmental and regulatory approvals. There can be no assurances when or if these approvals will be obtained.

North Fork Rancheria of Mono Indian Tribe

The Company has entered into Development and Management Agreements with the North Fork Rancheria of Mono Indians (the "Mono"), a federally recognized Native American tribe located near Fresno, California. Pursuant to those agreements, the Company will assist the Mono in developing and operating a gaming and entertainment facility to be located in Madera County, California. The Company has secured for the benefit of the Mono two parcels of land located on Highway 99 north of the city of Madera. Under the terms of the

Development Agreement, the Company has agreed to arrange the financing for the ongoing development costs and construction of the facility. Funds advanced by the Company are expected to be repaid from the proceeds of the project financing or from the Mono's gaming revenues. As of December 31, 2004, the Company had advanced approximately $1.5 million toward the development of this project, primarily to secure real estate for future development, which is included in other assets, net on the Company's consolidated balance sheets. In addition, the Company has agreed to pay approximately $1.3 million of payments upon achieving certain milestones, which will not be reimbursed. As of December 31, 2004, none of these payments had been made. The Management Agreement has a term of seven years from the opening of the facility and provides for a management fee of 24% of the facility's net income. As currently contemplated, the facility will include approximately 2,000 slot machines, 60 table games, dining, hotel and entertainment amenities. Development of the gaming and entertainment project is subject to certain governmental and regulatory approvals, including, but not limited to, negotiating a gaming compact with the State of California, the DOI accepting the land into trust on behalf of the Mono and approval of the Management Agreement by the NIGC. Prior to obtaining third-party financing, the Company will contribute significant financial support to the project. The timing of this type of project is difficult to predict and is dependent upon the receipt of the necessary gonernmental and regulatory approvals. There can be no assurances when or if these approvals will be obtained.

11. OTHER

Cash Transaction Reporting Violations

In April 2003, the Company became aware of violations of certain gaming regulations regarding the reporting of certain cash transactions. The Company self-reported these violations to the Nevada State Gaming Control Board. The Company, along with the Nevada State Gaming Control Board, has investigated the violations. On September 24, 2004, the Nevada Gaming Commission approved the settlement agreement in which we paid approximately $2.4 million in fines and investigative costs to the State of Nevada. The Company has hired additional staff at each of its properties and has increased the level of internal audit review to prevent this type of violation in the future.

12. STOCKHOLDERS' EQUITY

Common Stock

The Company is authorized to issue up to 135 million shares of its common stock, $0.01 par value per share, 77,298,227 shares of which were issued and 10,185,343 shares of which were held in treasury as of December 31, 2004. Each holder of the common stock is entitled to one vote for each share held of record on each matter submitted to a vote of stockholders. Holders of the common stock have no cumulative voting, conversion, redemption or preemptive rights or other rights to subscribe for additional shares other than pursuant to the Rights Plan described below. Subject to any preferences that may be granted to the holders of the Company's preferred stock, each holder of common stock is entitled to receive ratably, such dividends as may be declared by the Board of Directors out of funds legally available therefore, as well as any distributions to the stockholders and, in the event of liquidation, dissolution or winding up of the Company, is entitled to share ratably in all assets of the Company remaining after payment of liabilities.

During the year ended December 31, 2004, the Company paid a quarterly cash dividend of $0.125 per share to shareholders of record on February 12, 2004, $0.175 per share to shareholders of record on May 14, 2004 and August 13, 2004 and $0.21 per share to shareholders of record on November 12, 2004. The total amount paid in dividends for 2004 was $44.3 million. During the year ended December 31, 2003, the Company paid a quarterly cash dividend of $0.125 per share to shareholders of record on August 14, 2003 and November 13, 2003 for a total of $14.9 million.

Preferred Stock

The Company is authorized to issue up to 5 million shares of its preferred stock, $0.01 par value per share of which none were issued. The Board of Directors, without further action by the holders of common stock, may issue shares of preferred stock in one or more series and may fix or alter the rights, preferences, privileges and restrictions, including the voting rights, redemption provisions (including sinking fund provisions), dividend rights, dividend rates, liquidation rates, liquidation preferences, conversion rights and the description and number of shares constituting any wholly unissued series of preferred stock. Except as described above, the Board of Directors, without further stockholder approval, may issue shares of preferred stock with rights that could adversely affect the rights of the holders of common stock. The issuance of shares of preferred stock under certain circumstances could have the effect of delaying or preventing a change of control of the Company or other corporate action.

Treasury Stock

During the year ended December 31, 2004, the Company repurchased approximately 64,000 shares of its common stock for approximately $3.2 million. The Company is authorized to repurchase up to approximately 19.5 million shares of its common stock. As of December 31, 2004, the Company had acquired approximately 10.2 million shares at a cost of approximately $137.7 million.

Other Comprehensive Income

SFAS No. 130, "Reporting Comprehensive Income", requires companies to disclose other comprehensive income and the components of such income. Comprehensive income is the total of net income and all other non-stockholder changes in equity. For the years ended December 31, 2004, 2003 and 2002, the Company recorded its 50% interest in the mark-to-market valuation of the interest rate swaps at Green Valley Ranch Station as other comprehensive income (loss). Comprehensive income was computed as follows (amounts in thousands):

	For the years ended December 31,		
	2004	2003	2002
Net income	$ 66,350	$ 44,343	$ 17,932
Mark-to-market valuation of interest rate swaps, net of tax	723	361	(1,695)
Comprehensive income	$ 67,073	$ 44,704	$ 16,237

Rights Plan

On October 6, 1997, the Company declared a dividend of one preferred share purchase right (a "Right") for each outstanding share of common stock. The dividend was paid on October 21, 1997. Each Right entitles the registered holder to purchase from the Company one one-hundredth of a share of Series A Preferred Stock, par value $0.01 per share ("Preferred Shares") of the Company at a price of $40.00 per one one-hundredth of a Preferred Share, subject to adjustment. The Rights are not exercisable until the earlier of 10 days following a public announcement that a person or group of affiliated or associated persons have acquired beneficial ownership of 15% or more of the outstanding common stock ("Acquiring Person") or 10 business days (or such later date as may be determined by action of the Board of Directors prior to such time as any person or group of affiliated persons becomes an Acquiring Person) following the commencement of, or announcement of an intention to make, a tender offer or exchange offer, the consummation of which would result in the beneficial ownership by a person or group of 15% or more of the outstanding common stock.

The Rights will expire on October 21, 2007. Acquiring Persons do not have the same rights to receive common stock as other holders upon exercise of the Rights. Because of the nature of the Preferred Shares' dividend, liquidation and voting rights, the value of one one-hundredth interest in a Preferred Share purchasable upon exercise of each Right should approximate the value of one common share. In the event that any person or group of affiliated or associated persons becomes an Acquiring Person, the proper provisions will be made so that each holder of a Right, other than Rights beneficially owned by the Acquiring Person (which will thereafter become void), will thereafter have the right to receive upon exercise that number of shares of common stock having a market value of two times the exercise price of the Right. In the event that the Company is acquired in a merger or other business combination transaction or 50% or more of its consolidated assets or earning power are sold after a person or group has become an Acquiring Person, proper provision will be made so that each holder of a Right will thereafter have the right to receive, upon exercise thereof, that number of shares of common stock of the acquiring company, which at the time of such transaction will have a market value of two times the exercise price of the Right. Because of the characteristics of the Rights in connection with a person or group of affiliated or associated persons becoming an Acquiring Person, the Rights may have the effect of making an acquisition of the Company more difficult and may discourage such an acquisition.

13. Benefit Plans

Stock Compensation Programs

The Company has adopted a Stock Compensation Program which includes (i) an Incentive Stock Option Plan for the grant of incentive stock options, (ii) a Compensatory Stock Option Plan providing for the grant of nonqualified stock options, (iii) a Restricted Shares Plan providing for the grant of restricted shares of common stock and (iv) a Nonemployee Director Stock Option Plan, providing for the grant of nonqualified stock options. The Company has also adopted the 1999 Stock Compensation Program (combined with the Stock Compensation Program "the Programs"), which includes (i) the 1999 Compensatory Stock Option Plan providing for the majority of the grants of nonqualified stock options to employees who are not officers or directors of the Company and (ii) the 1999 Share Plan which grants shares of the Company's common stock to employees based on their length of service with the Company and restricted shares of common stock are granted. Officers, key employees, directors (whether employee or non-employee) and independent contractors or consultants of the Company and its subsidiaries are eligible to participate in the Programs. However, only employees of the Company and its subsidiaries are eligible to receive incentive stock options.

A maximum of 18,710,500 shares of common stock has been reserved for issuance under the Programs. Options are granted at the current market price at the date of grant. The plan provides for a variety of vesting schedules, including immediate, 20% per year for five years, 10% per year for 10 years, and a cliff vest at the vesting date, to be determined at the time of grant. Generally, all options expire 10 years from the date of grant.

The Programs will terminate 10 years from the date of adoption or extension, unless terminated earlier by the Board of Directors, and no options or restricted shares may be granted under the Programs after such date. Summarized information for the Programs is as follows:

| | | | | | | _For the years ended December 31,_ |
| | 2004 | | | 2003 | | | 2002 |
	Options	_Weighted average exercise price_	_Options_	_Weighted average exercise price_	_Options_	_Weighted average exercise price_
Outstanding at beginning of the year	9,619,816	$ 11.25	13,533,544	$ 10.59	14,637,783	$10.22
Granted	–	–	169,500	$ 19.98	1,649,500	$13.70
Exercised	(5,203,316)	$ 10.57	(3,838,986)	$ 8.63	(1,079,667)	$ 8.46
Canceled	(463,800)	$ 12.72	(244,242)	$ 13.15	(1,674,072)	$13.07
Outstanding at end of the year	3,952,700	$ 11.96	9,619,816	$ 11.25	13,533,544	$10.59
Exercisable at end of year	1,972,850	$ 11.82	5,383,469	$ 10.36	7,133,595	$ 9.05
Options available for grant	456,876		1,182,455		1,497,825	

The following table summarizes information about the options outstanding at December 31, 2004:

| | | _Options Outstanding_ | | | _Options Exercisable_ | |
Range of exercise prices	_Number outstanding at December 31, 2004_	_Weighted average remaining contractual life_	_Weighted average exercise price_	_Number exercisable at December 31, 2004_	_Weighted average exercise price_
$ 3.29 – $ 8.00	247,400	4.10	$ 5.72	205,600	$ 5.32
$ 8.01 – $ 16.00	3,486,450	6.40	$ 11.98	1,707,500	$ 12.39
$ 16.01 – $ 24.00	196,350	7.50	$ 17.62	57,250	$ 17.31
$ 24.01 – $ 31.65	22,500	8.70	$ 29.51	2,500	$ 31.23
	3,952,700	6.32	$ 11.96	1,972,850	$ 11.82

Restricted stock grants of 1,420,413, 383,468, and 50,000 shares were issued under the Programs during the years ended December 31, 2004, 2003 and 2002, respectively. The effect of these grants is to increase the issued and outstanding shares of the Company's common stock and decrease the number of shares available for grant in the plan. Deferred compensation is recorded for the restricted stock grants equal to the market value of the Company's common stock on the date of grant. The deferred compensation is amortized over the period the restricted stock vests and is recorded as compensation expense in the accompanying consolidated statements of operations.

The fair value on the grant date of the restricted shares and the amount of compensation expense recognized in connection with the restricted shares is as follows (amounts in thousands):

	For the years ended December 31,		
	2004	2003	2002
Fair value on grant date	$ 65,924	$ 11,472	$ 695
Compensation expense	9,676	3,201	2,973

401(k) Plan

The Company has a defined contribution 401(k) plan, which covers all employees who meet certain age and length of service requirements and allows an employer contribution up to 50% of the first 4% of each participating employee's compensation. Plan participants can elect to defer before tax compensation through payroll deductions. These deferrals are regulated under Section 401(k) of the Internal Revenue Code. The Company's matching contribution was approximately $2.0 million, $1.8 million and $1.7 million for the years ended December 31, 2004, 2003 and 2002, respectively.

14. EXECUTIVE COMPENSATION PLANS

The Company has employment agreements with certain of its executive officers. These contracts provide for, among other things, an annual base salary, supplemental long-term disability and supplemental life insurance benefits in excess of the Company's normal coverage for employees. In addition, the Company has adopted a Supplemental Executive Retirement Plan for its Chief Executive Officer and President and a Supplemental Management Retirement Plan for certain key executives as selected by the Governance and Compensation Committee of the Company's Board of Directors. Other executive plans include a Deferred Compensation Plan and a Long-Term Stay-On Performance Incentive Plan.

15. Income Taxes

The Company files a consolidated federal income tax return. The provision for income taxes for financial reporting purposes consists of the following (amounts in thousands):

	For the years ended December 31,		
	2004	2003	2002
Income tax provision from continuing operations	$ (38,879)	$ (23,834)	$ (18,508)
Tax benefit from change in accounting principle	--	--	7,170
Total income taxes	$ (38,879)	$ (23,834)	$ (11,338)

The provision for income taxes attributable to net income consists of the following (amounts in thousands):

	For the years ended December 31,		
	2004	2003	2002
Current	$ (10,187)	$ (27,416)	$ (2,852)
Deferred	(28,692)	3,582	(15,656)
Total income taxes	$ (38,879)	$ (23,834)	$ (18,508)

The income tax provision differs from that computed at the federal statutory corporate tax rate as follows:

	For the years ended December 31,		
	2004	2003	2002
Federal statutory rate	35.0%	35.0%	35.0%
Lobbying and political	0.4	0.2	0.7
Fines & penalties	0.6	--	--
Meals and entertainment	0.1	0.1	0.6
Credits earned, net	(0.6)	(0.9)	(1.7)
Nondeductible officers compensation	2.4	2.6	2.8
Reduction in liability based on conclusion of an IRS examination	(1.1)	(2.2)	--
Other, net	0.1	0.2	1.3
Effective Tax Rate	36.9%	35.0%	38.7%

The tax effects of significant temporary differences representing net deferred tax assets and liabilities are as follows (amounts in thousands):

	December 31,	
	2004	2003
Deferred tax assets:		
Accrued vacation, bonuses and group insurance	$ 4,986	$ 3,880
Preopening and other costs, net of amortization	4,991	4,434
Net operating loss carryover	53,256	–
Accrued benefits	13,739	11,614
FICA credits	2,846	1,179
Minimum tax credit carryover	20,838	19,999
Other deferred tax assets	5,294	18,253
TOTAL DEFERRED TAX ASSETS	$ 105,950	$ 59,359
Deferred tax liabilities:		
Prepaid expenses and other	$ (10,463)	$ (5,329)
Temporary differences related to property and equipment	(110,309)	(100,027)
Amortization	(5,485)	(1,150)
Other	–	(1,334)
TOTAL DEFERRED TAX LIABILITIES	$ (126,257)	$ (107,840)
Net	$ (20,307)	$ (48,481)

The excess of the tentative minimum tax over the regular federal income tax is a tax credit, which can be carried forward indefinitely to reduce future regular federal income tax liabilities. The Company did not record a valuation allowance at December 31, 2004 or 2003 relating to recorded tax benefits because all benefits are more likely than not to be realized.

During 2004 and 2003, the Internal Revenue Service ("IRS") completed their audits through and including December 31, 2002. Based on the favorable conclusion of their audits, the Company recorded a reduction in its tax contingency reserve of approximately $1.1 million and $1.5 million in the years ended December 31, 2004 and 2003, respectively.

As of December 31, 2004, the Company has a tax net operating loss carryover of approximately $152 million that expires in 2024. SFAS No. 109 requires that the tax benefit of a net operating loss be recorded as an asset. Management believes that the realization of this deferred tax asset is more likely than not based on expectations of future taxable income.

As of December 31, 2004, the Company has a capital loss carryover of approximately $85 thousand that is available to offset capital gains. SFAS No. 109 requires that the tax benefit of a capital loss be recorded as an asset. Management believes that the realization of this deferred tax asset is more likely than not based on the characterization of taxable income.

16. LEGAL MATTERS

The Company and its subsidiaries are defendants in various lawsuits relating to routine matters incidental to their business. As with all litigation, no assurance can be provided as to the outcome of the following matters and litigation inherently involves significant costs. Following is a summary of key litigation impacting the Company.

Poulos/Ahearn Litigation

On April 26, 1994, a suit seeking status as a class action lawsuit was filed by plaintiff, William H. Poulos, et al., as class representative, in the United States District Court for the Middle District of Florida (the "Florida District Court"), naming 41 manufacturers, distributors and casino operators of video poker and electronic slot machines, including Station Casinos. On May 10, 1994, a lawsuit alleging substantially identical claims was filed by another plaintiff, William Ahearn, et al., as class representative, in the Florida District Court against 48 manufacturers, distributors and casino operators of video poker and electronic slot machines, including the Company and most of the other major hotel/casino companies. The lawsuits allege that the defendants have engaged in a course of fraudulent and misleading conduct intended to induce persons to play such games based on a false belief concerning how the gaming machines operate, as well as the extent to which there is an opportunity to win. The two lawsuits have been consolidated into a single action, and have been transferred to the United States District Court for the District of Nevada (the "Nevada District Court"). On September 26, 1995, a lawsuit alleging substantially identical claims was filed by plaintiff, Larry Schreier, et al., as class representative, in the Nevada District Court, naming 45 manufacturers, distributors, and casino operators of video poker and electronic slot machines, including the Company. Motions to dismiss the Poulos/Ahearn and Schreier cases were filed by defendants. On April 17, 1996, the Poulos/Ahearn lawsuits were dismissed, but plaintiffs were given leave to file Amended Complaints on or before May 31, 1996. On May 31, 1996, an Amended Complaint was filed, naming William H. Poulos, et al., as plaintiff. Defendants filed a motion to dismiss. On August 15, 1996, the Schreier lawsuit was dismissed with leave to amend. On September 27, 1996, Schreier filed an Amended Complaint. Defendants filed motions to dismiss the Amended Complaint. In December 1996, the Nevada District Court consolidated the Poulos/Ahearn, the Schreier, and a third case not involving the Company and ordered all pending motions be deemed withdrawn without prejudice, including Defendants' Motions to Dismiss the Amended Complaints. The plaintiffs filed a Consolidated Amended Complaint on February 13, 1997. On or about December 19, 1997, the Nevada District Court issued formal opinions granting in part and denying in part the defendants' motion to dismiss. In so doing, the Nevada District Court ordered plaintiffs to file an amended complaint in accordance with the Court's orders in January of 1998. Accordingly, plaintiffs amended their complaint and filed it with the Nevada District Court in February 1998. The Company and all other defendants continue to deny the allegations contained in the amended complaint filed on behalf of plaintiffs. The plaintiffs are seeking compensatory, special, consequential, incidental, and punitive damages in unspecified amounts.

On June 25, 2002, the Nevada District Court denied plaintiffs' motion for class certification. On July 11, 2002, plaintiffs filed a petition for permission to appeal such class certification ruling with the United States Court of Appeals for the Ninth Circuit. On August 15, 2002, the Ninth Circuit granted the plaintiffs' petition for permission to appeal such class certification ruling. On January 15, 2004, the Court of Appeals heard oral argument on this matter. On August 10, 2004, the Ninth Circuit affirmed the District Court's order denying the plaintiff's motion for class certification. Accordingly, the matter is scheduled to move forward on behalf of the three named plaintiffs only. While no assurances can be made with respect to any litigation, the Company believes that the plaintiffs' claims are without merit and does not expect that the lawsuits will have a material adverse effect on the Company's financial position or results of operations.

Harrah's Litigation

On July 13, 2001, the Company and five of its major operating subsidiaries were named as defendants in a lawsuit brought by Harrah's Entertainment, Inc. and Harrah's Operating Company, Inc. in the United States District Court, District of Nevada (CV-S-01-0825-PMP-RJJ). The plaintiffs allege that the Company and its subsidiaries are liable for unspecified actual and punitive damages, and they seek injunctive and other relief, based on allegations that the Company's "Boarding Pass Rewards Program" infringes on various patents held by the plaintiffs.

On October 4, 2001, the Company and the subsidiaries filed their answer and counterclaim seeking declaratory judgment that Harrah's patents (1) are not infringed by the Company's and the subsidiaries' actions, (2) are invalid under federal patent law and (3) are rendered unenforceable due to Harrah's inequitable conduct. On March 27, 2002, Harrah's filed an amended complaint, which added an additional defendant, Green Valley Ranch Gaming, LLC, which is an affiliate of the Company. On April 22, 2002, the Company and its subsidiaries and affiliate filed their amended answer and counterclaim denying infringement by Green Valley Ranch Gaming, LLC, and alleging Harrah's committed further acts of inequitable conduct.

On January 17, 2003, the Company filed motions for summary judgment or partial summary judgment on several issues: (1) a Motion for Summary Judgment of Patent Unenforceability Due To Inequitable Conduct, (2) a Motion for Summary Judgment of Patent Invalidity Under 35 U.S.C. ss 102 and 103 (lack of novelty and obviousness), (3) a Motion for Partial Summary Judgment of Patent Invalidity Under 35 U.S.C. s 112 (indefiniteness, lack of written description and failure to disclose best mode), (4) a Motion for Partial Summary Judgment of Non-Infringement of U.S. Patent No. 6,003,013, and (5) a Motion for Partial Summary Judgment of Non-Infringement of U.S. Patent No. 6,183,362. That same day, Harrah's filed motions for partial summary judgment on several issues: (1) a Motion for Partial Summary Judgment of Infringement of Claims 15-18 of U.S. Patent No. 5,761,647, (2) a Motion for Partial Summary Judgment of Infringement of Claims 1-2 and 49 of U.S. Patent No. 6,003,013, (3) a Motion for Partial Summary Judgment on Defendants' Invalidity Defenses, and (4) a Motion for Partial Summary Judgment That Certain Third Party Systems Are Not Prior Art. During February and March of 2003, the parties filed oppositions, reply briefs and various motions to strike in response to the summary judgment motions.

On March 23, 2004, the District Court heard oral argument on certain of the summary judgment motions and motions to strike. On May 19, 2004, the District Court granted the Company's motion for summary judgment on Harrah's claims that the Company had infringed upon U.S. Patents Nos. 5,761,647 and 6,183,362, held by Harrah's relating to its customer rewards and tracking program. In granting that motion, the District Court ruled that such patents are invalid as a matter of law due to indefiniteness and lack of enabling disclosure of the claimed subject matter. A substantial portion of the patent infringement claim brought by Harrah's regarding U.S. Patent No. 6,003,013 (the "013 Patent") was also dismissed as a result of that summary judgment ruling. On August 23, 2004, the District Court entered final judgment and declared invalid all claims of U.S. Patent Nos. 5,761,647 and 6,183,362, and all but three claims of the '013 Patent. The final judgment also dismissed with prejudice all claims of the '013 Patent that were not declared invalid, and dismissed without prejudice the Company's counterclaims for declaratory judgment of noninfringement and invalidity.

On September 13, 2004, Harrah's filed a Notice of Appeal with the United States Court of Appeals for the Federal Circuit. On October 14, 2004, the Company filed a Notice of Cross Appeal with the Federal Circuit. On February 17, 2005, Harrah's filed its appellate brief with the Federal Circuit. While no assurances can be made with respect to any litigation, the Company believes that the plaintiffs' claims are without merit and does not expect that the lawsuit will have a material adverse effect on its financial position or results of operations.

Plattner Litigation

On May 2, 2003, the Company and one of its operating subsidiaries, Palace Station Hotel & Casino, Inc. ("Palace Station"), were named as defendants in a lawsuit seeking status as a class action brought by Dov Plattner in the Superior Court of Los Angeles County, California (Case No. CB295056).

The lawsuit seeks to recover for alleged breach of contract, fraud, negligent misrepresentation, breach of covenant of good faith and fair dealing, promissory fraud, unjust enrichment and violations of sections 17200 and 17500, et. seq. of the California Business and Professions Code, all in connection with energy and telephone surcharge fees imposed on Palace Station hotel guests. The plaintiff is requesting unspecified actual and punitive damages, as well as injunctive and other relief.

On November 10, 2003, the defendants filed a response to the complaint denying all liability. On June 18, 2004, the parties entered into a Settlement Agreement and Release (the "Proposed Settlement"). Pursuant to the Proposed Settlement and subject to Superior Court approval, the parties have agreed that the Company will (i) issue two personalized coupons to each Settlement Class Member (as defined in the Proposed Settlement), one for $3.00 and one for $2.50, with each coupon to be good toward a discount of a quoted room rate for a single night's stay at any of the Station Hotels (as defined in the Proposed Settlement), and (ii) pay the plaintiff's reasonable attorneys' fees and expenses in exchange for the plaintiff dismissing the lawsuit (including all claims held by the members of the settlement class and the general public) with prejudice. The Proposed Settlement stipulates that the Company denies any liability with respect to the plaintiff's claims. On October 22, 2004, the Superior Court approved the Proposed Settlement and dismissed the lawsuit with prejudice, except for the claims of eight class members that opted out of the settlement class.

Castillo Litigation

On May 14, 2003, the Company (as a nominal defendant only) and all of its executive officers and directors were named as defendants in a derivative action lawsuit, which also seeks status as a class action, brought by Bernard Castillo in the District Court of Clark County, Nevada (Case No. A467663).

The lawsuit alleges that (1) the director defendants breached their fiduciary duties by failing to make certain disclosures in the Company's 2002 Proxy Statement regarding the sale by the Company of its subsidiary, Southwest Gaming Services, Inc. ("SGSI"), and regarding a proposal seeking shareholder approval of an amendment to the Company's stock option plan; (2) the director defendants breached their fiduciary duties in approving the sale of SGSI and in recommending approval of the option plan amendment; and (3) the purchasers of SGSI and the recipients of certain benefits made possible by the option plan amendment were unjustly enriched. The plaintiff is requesting unspecified actual damages, as well as injunctive and other relief.

On July 21, 2003, the defendants filed a motion to dismiss or, in the alternative, motion to stay all of the plaintiff's claims. On October 24, 2003, the District Court granted the motion to stay all of plaintiff's claims pending the consideration of such claims by a special litigation committee to be formed by the Company in accordance with the Court's order granting such motion. On November 19, 2003, the defendants filed their first amended answer to the complaint. On February 27, 2004, the District Court entered another order extending the stay for another 120 days pending the special litigation committee investigation.

On July 9, 2004, the parties entered into a Stipulation of Settlement (the "Proposed Settlement"). Pursuant to the Proposed Settlement and subject to District Court approval, the parties have agreed that the Company will (i) adopt new language in its Corporate Governance Guidelines, which specifically relates to "interested director transactions," and (ii) pay the plaintiff's attorneys' fees and expenses in exchange for the plaintiff dismissing the lawsuit (including all claims held by the Company and the members of the certified class), with prejudice. The Proposed Settlement stipulates that the Company denies any liability with respect to the plaintiff's claims. On September 13, 2004, the District Court approved the Proposed Settlement and dismissed the lawsuit with prejudice.

17. QUARTERLY FINANCIAL INFORMATION (UNAUDITED)

(amounts in thousands, except per share amounts)	Net revenues	Operating income	Income (loss) before income taxes and change in accounting principle	Net income (loss) applicable to common stock	Diluted earnings (loss) per common share
Year ended December 31, 2004					
First quarter (a)	$ 238,965	$ 63,651	$ (46,497)	$ (29,758)	$ (0.48)
Second quarter (b)	240,177	62,328	45,328	29,010	0.43
Third quarter (c)	242,862	58,608	45,670	29,086	0.43
Fourth quarter (d)	264,738	72,468	60,728	38,012	0.55
Year ended December 31, 2003					
First quarter (e)	$ 199,561	$ 40,550	$ 19,938	$ 12,561	$ 0.21
Second quarter (f)	210,005	48,002	32,743	20,628	0.33
Third quarter (g)	218,670	49,880	31,431	19,802	0.32
Fourth quarter (h)	229,853	2,639	(15,935)	(8,648)	(0.14)

(a) Includes development expense of approximately $4.0 million and loss on early retirement of debt of approximately $93.3 million.

(b) Includes development expense of approximately $2.2 million and preopening expense of approximately $0.3 million.

(c) Includes development expense of approximately $2.1 million and preopening expense of approximately $0.3 million.

(d) Includes development expenses of approximately $2.4 million and preopening expense of approximately $0.3 million.

(e) Includes an impairment loss of approximately $1.4 million primarily related to the write-off of an investment in the development of a new slot product (see Note 7).

(f) Includes development fees of approximately $3.6 million from Thunder Valley.

(g) Includes development fees of approximately $0.8 million from Thunder Valley. Also includes development expenses of approximately $2.9 million.

(h) Includes development fees of approximately $0.2 million from Thunder Valley, development expenses of approximately $1.4 million, a goodwill impairment loss of approximately $17.5 million at Fiesta Rancho (see Goodwill and Other Intangibles in Note 1) and a litigation settlement of $38.0 million.

MANAGEMENT'S REPORT ON INTERNAL CONTROL OVER FINANCIAL REPORTING

The management of the Company is responsible for establishing and maintaining adequate internal control over financial reporting. The Company's internal control system was designed to provide reasonable assurance to the Company's management and board of directors regarding the preparation and fair presentation of published financial statements.

All internal control systems, no matter how well designed, have inherent limitations, including the possibility of human error and the circumvention or overriding of controls. Accordingly, even effective internal controls can provide only reasonable assurances with respect to financial statement preparation. Further because of changes in conditions, the effectiveness of internal controls may vary over time.

Management assessed the effectiveness of the company's internal control over financial reporting as of December 31, 2004. In making this assessment, it used the criteria set forth by the Committee of Sponsoring Organizations of the Treadway Commission (COSO) in Internal Control – Integrated Framework. Based on our assessment we believe that, as of December 31, 2004, the Company's internal control over financial reporting is effective based on those criteria.

The Company's independent auditors have issued an audit report on our assessment of the company's internal control over financial reporting. This report appears on page 140.

REPORT OF INDEPENDENT REGISTERED PUBLIC ACCOUNTING FIRM

To the Board of Directors and Stockholders of the Station Casinos, Inc.:

We have audited the accompanying consolidated balance sheets of Station Casinos, Inc. and its subsidiaries (the "Company") as of December 31, 2004 and 2003 and the related consolidated statements of operations, stockholders' equity and cash flows for each of the two years in the period ended December 31, 2004. These financial statements are the responsibility of the Company's management. Our responsibility is to express an opinion on these financial statements based on our audits.

We conducted our audits in accordance with the standards of the Public Company Accounting Oversight Board (United States). Those standards require that we plan and perform the audit to obtain reasonable assurance about whether the financial statements are free of material misstatement. An audit includes examining, on a test basis, evidence supporting the amounts and disclosures in the financial statements. An audit also includes assessing the accounting principles used and significant estimates made by management, as well as evaluating the overall financial statement presentation. We believe that our audits provide a reasonable basis for our opinion.

In our opinion, the financial statements referred to above present fairly, in all material respects, the consolidated financial position of the Company at December 31, 2004 and 2003, and the consolidated results of their operations and their cash flows for each of the two years in the period ended December 31, 2004, in conformity with accounting principles generally accepted in the United States.

We also have audited, in accordance with the standards of the Public Company Accounting Oversight Board (United States), the effectiveness of the Company's internal control over financial reporting as of December 31, 2004, based on criteria established in Internal Control – Integrated Framework issued by the Committee of Sponsoring Organizations of the Treadway Commission and our report dated February 18, 2005 expressed an unqualified opinion thereon.

/s/Ernst & Young LLP

Las Vegas, Nevada
February 18, 2005

Report of Independent Registered Public Accounting Firm

The Board of Directors and Stockholders of Station Casinos, Inc.:

We have audited management's assessment, included in the accompanying Management's Report on Internal Control Over Financial Reporting (see page 138), that Station Casinos Inc. and its subsidiaries (the "Company") maintained effective internal control over financial reporting as of December 31, 2004, based on criteria established in Internal Control – Integrated Framework issued by the Committee of Sponsoring Organizations of the Treadway Commission (the COSO criteria). The Company's management is responsible for maintaining effective internal control over financial reporting and for its assessment of the effectiveness of internal control over financial reporting. Our responsibility is to express an opinion on management's assessment and an opinion on the effectiveness of the Company's internal control over financial reporting based on our audit.

We conducted our audit in accordance with the standards of the Public Company Accounting Oversight Board (United States). Those standards require that we plan and perform the audit to obtain reasonable assurance about whether effective internal control over financial reporting was maintained in all material respects. Our audit included obtaining an understanding of internal control over financial reporting, evaluating management's assessment, testing and evaluating the design and operating effectiveness of internal control, and performing such other procedures as we considered necessary in the circumstances. We believe that our audit provides a reasonable basis for our opinion.

A company's internal control over financial reporting is a process designed to provide reasonable assurance regarding the reliability of financial reporting and the preparation of financial statements for external purposes in accordance with generally accepted accounting principles. A company's internal control over financial reporting includes those policies and procedures that (1) pertain to the maintenance of records that, in reasonable detail, accurately and fairly reflect the transactions and dispositions of the assets of the company; (2) provide reasonable assurance that transactions are recorded as necessary to permit preparation of financial statements in accordance with generally accepted accounting principles, and that receipts and expenditures of the company are being made only in accordance with authorizations of management and directors of the company; and (3) provide reasonable assurance regarding prevention or timely detection of unauthorized acquisition, use, or disposition of the company's assets that could have a material effect on the financial statements.

Because of its inherent limitations, internal control over financial reporting may not prevent or detect misstatements. Also, projections of any evaluation of effectiveness to future periods are subject to the risk that controls may become inadequate because of changes in conditions, or that the degree of compliance with the policies or procedures may deteriorate.

In our opinion, management's assessment that the Company maintained effective internal control over financial reporting as of December 31, 2004, is fairly stated, in all material respects, based on the COSO criteria. Also, in our opinion, the Company maintained, in all material respects, effective internal control over financial reporting as of December 31, 2004, based on the COSO criteria.

We also have audited, in accordance with the standards of the Public Company Accounting Oversight Board, the consolidated balance sheets of the Company as of December 31, 2004 and 2003, and the related consolidated statements of operations, stockholders' equity, and cash flows for each of the two years in the period ended December 31, 2004 of the Company and our report dated February 18, 2005 expressed an unqualified opinion thereon.

/s/Ernst & Young LLP

Las Vegas, Nevada

REPORT OF INDEPENDENT REGISTERED PUBLIC ACCOUNTING FIRM

To the Board of Directors and Stockholders of Station Casinos, Inc.:

We have audited the accompanying consolidated statements of operations, stockholders' equity and cash flows of Station Casinos, Inc. and subsidiaries (the "Company") (a Nevada corporation) for the year ended December 31, 2002. These financial statements are the responsibility of the Company's management. Our responsibility is to express an opinion on these financial statements based on our audit.

We conducted our audit in accordance with standards of the Public Company Accounting Oversight Board (United States). Those standards require that we plan and perform the audit to obtain reasonable assurance about whether the financial statements are free of material misstatement. An audit includes examining, on a test basis, evidence supporting the amounts and disclosures in the financial statements. An audit also includes assessing the accounting principles used and significant estimates made by management, as well as evaluating the overall financial statement presentation. We believe that our audit provides a reasonable basis for our opinion.

In our opinion, such consolidated financial statements present fairly, in all material respects, the results of operations and cash flows of Station Casinos, Inc. and subsidiaries for the year ended December 31, 2002 in conformity with accounting principles generally accepted in the United States of America.

As discussed in Note 1 to the consolidated financial statements, in 2002, the Company changed its method of accounting for goodwill and other intangible assets to conform to Statement of Financial Accounting Standards No. 142, "Goodwill and Other Intangibles," and recorded a cumulative effect of a change in accounting principle in the first quarter of 2002.

Deloitte & Touche LLP
Las Vegas, Nevada
January 29, 2003

Index

About the Author

Dr. Wayne A. Label, CPA, MBA, PhD, was born and raised in San Francisco. He completed his undergraduate work in accounting at the University of California, Berkeley and then went on to the University of California, Los Angeles where he received his MBA and a PhD in accounting. He is a Certified Public Accountant in the state of Texas.

He has taught at several universities in the United States and abroad. He was the Director of the School of Accountancy at the University of Hawaii and chairman of the accounting department at the University of Nevada, Las Vegas. Dr. Label also taught for the Harvard Institute of International Development where he helped to start the Master's Degree Program in Auditing in La Paz, Bolivia. He received a Ford Foundation grant to aid the beginning of an MBA program at the Catholic University in Rio de Janeiro, Brazil. He has also taught accounting courses in Peru, Chile, Mexico, and Germany.

Dr. Label has published three books on accounting, and over thirty articles in professional journals. He is currently teaching online courses for the University of Maryland University College and UCLA. Dr. Label has also given seminars in accounting and international business in numerous locations throughout the United States, as well as in Latin America, Europe, and Asia.

Dr. Label divides his time between Puerto Vallarta, Mexico, and San Diego, California.

You can learn more about Dr. Label at his website: www.waynelabel.com. He can be contacted at wayne@waynelabel.com.